THE CARPENTER PATRIOT

*How leftism seeks to kill the workingman
and erase common sense*

WILL HOLLADAY

W&H PUBLISHERS

All photographs by the author
Portrait of Bill Michel drawn by Kay Kristenson
The following versions of the Holy Bible are used in quotations:
American Standard Version (ASV) – public domain.
New International Version (NIV). Copyright © 1973, 1978, 1984, 2011 by Biblica,Inc.™.
All rights reserved. Used by permission.

ISBN-13: 978-0-945186-08-3

Library of Congress Catalog Card Number: 2017918685
Printed in the United States of America.

W&H Publishers
Minersville, PA

Cover photo: An American Indian gazes out over Central AZ from the Mogollon Rim

DEDICATED TO ALL THOSE BRAVE MEN AND WOMEN OF THE US
ARMED FORCES WHO GAVE THEIR LIVES, SACRIFICED THEIR LIMBS,
AND SHED THEIR BLOOD SO THAT I CAN LIVE AS A FREE MAN

Books by Will Holladay

A Roof Cutter's Secrets to Framing the Custom Home
The Complicated Roof – A Cut and Stack Workbook
From the Top Plates Up – A Production Roof Framer's Journey
The Carpenter Patriot

Videos by Will Holladay

A Roof Cutter's Secrets – live workshop
Roof framing for the Professional – The Essentials
Roof Framing for the Professional – Advanced Topics

Contents

Introduction

"It is seldom that liberty of any kind is lost all at once. Slavery has so frightful an aspect to men accustomed to freedom that it must steal in upon them by degrees and must disguise itself in a thousand shapes in order to be received." – David Hume

WHEN YOU READ ABOUT the players who participated in the December 16, 1773 Boston Tea Party, you come to find out that about 1 in 3 of them were tradesmen. The USA has come a long way from those first days, but I believe that the "hands on" hard-working folks are still some of the staunchest patriots to be found. I am proud to say that I am in that group. I am a Christian first, patriot second, and carpenter third.

James Burnham, in his 1964 book entitled *Suicide of the West*, states that "**Liberalism (leftism) is the ideology of Western suicide.**" He was dead on. Over my lifetime, I have seen this country fall away from the principles that made her great. It began with a distancing from the Biblical truths that had been set as the plumb line. Leftism with its propagation of existentialism has fought to blur any line between right and wrong. The character of the country has suffered as a result. It has fallen to the moral level of a slummy, Third World country. Lying and cheating are now commonplace. Everybody is now a "victim" of something. Frivolous lawsuits choke our court system. People refuse to take responsibility for their own lives and a welfare state "give me" mentality has become engrained

1

in our society. *"Our Constitution was made only for a moral and religious people. It is wholly inadequate to the government of any other."* – John Adams 1798

American history and economics are two subjects I have always found intriguing. I always wonder if I would have had the guts and fortitude of the early frontiersmen who claimed this country or if I could have made it as a modern day Army Delta or Navy SEAL special forces type soldier. We will never know and the odds are that I would never have cut the mustard, but I do enjoy reading about these "real" men with solid character. I have quite the collection of books written by our country's warriors and always keep my eyes open for more in the thrift stores. These "in the trenches" books have helped me get a grasp on history and the pain, misery, and suffering of war. They have also helped me develop a good deal of respect for our war veterans and, in particular, for a father I barely knew. From what I have heard, he was a brilliant, charismatic leader through his time in the armed forces and as manager of the flight systems division at North American Aviation. He was also quite the athlete, playing some college basketball at Georgia Tech where he got his Bachelors in Electrical Engineering (Masters at UCLA). He was part of the Navy ROTC program and served as a UDT (underwater demolition team) frogman in Korea. Sounds like they principally did mine sweeping, behind the lines info gathering, and clearing the beaches for troop insertion. His "bar fighting" buddy was Dick Bonin, who later went on to form Scuba Pro. At North American Aviation from 1954 to 1979, he worked on the designs of many aircraft, the most notorious being the X15, XF-108 Rapier, NA265 Saberliner, XB-70 Valkyrie, B1 Lancer, and the Space Shuttle. He and my mother never got along (some women should never marry), so I rarely had the chance to see him as a kid. Only later when I moved down to Los Angeles to attend the construction technology program at Orange

Coast College did I have the opportunity to spend some time with him. He played a major role in my conversion to Christianity and died in 1979, at only 51 years of age.

I tried briefly to follow in my father's footsteps as a military man and was accepted into the US Military Academy in 1974. I had kept fairly good grades through high school, was a decent athlete, and the local contractor for whom I worked knew the local state representative so I got the nod. My long-term plan was to make it into the Special Forces, but the Academy informed me that with my vision problems this was not an option. Disillusioned, and being somewhat of a rebellious turd, it wasn't long before I was separated from the other cadets and politely sent back to civilian life. It probably would have done me some real good to have stayed in, but at that time I wasn't mature enough to see the benefits or consider compromising my goal. In the end, I threw away an excellent opportunity. Who knows, I might have done OK in the Army Corps of Engineers or the Navy Seabees.

Bush pilot "Wild Bill" Michel, whom I met in Alaska while flying beach-caught Sockeye Salmon to the processor from the west side of the Kvichak River in 1993, was instrumental in opening my eyes to modern day Patriotism. He spent endless hours explaining how our freedoms have been enchained and slowly eroded since the Progressive movement beganin earnest with Woodrow Wilson in 1913, through FDR, L.B. Johnson, Jimmy Carter, etc. The setbacks this movement has caused to our liberty are never detailed in the mainstream media, so it must be learned by personal investigation. I ordered all kinds of books to study. One of my favorites is *Freedom in Chains* by James Bovard. Then again I love Milton Freedman's *Free to Choose*, Irwin Schiff's *The Kingdom of Moltz*, Mark Levin's *Liberty and Tyranny*, and Thomas Sowell's *Basic Economics*, just to name a few.

There is a popular saying which I am sure all of you know that states one should "never talk politics and religion with friends or family." That may be good advice, but I have always been a maverick, so why would I change now. I must be truthful to who I am. So, in this book I have chosen to share a bit about the political issues on which I am most passionate. I have seen our freedoms greatly diminished in my lifetime, and all of this certainly runs over into the life of a carpenter. I did not go about writing this book lightly, but spent an infinite amount of hours researching it from different angles so as to give credence to my actual real-life experience and exposure. I am an intensely logical guy and this is probably why I love economics so much. You may agree with my conclusions, or you may not, but either way you can always count on my friendship. I have faced opposition and controversy all my life, so when others think differently than I do, it doesn't faze me at all. Some of my very best friends hold opinions that are 180° opposite of mine. I do realize that no amount of facts and logic will ever change their minds, but still I try if an opportunity ever presents itself. *"Never underestimate the difficulty of changing false beliefs by facts."* – Henry Rosovsky. So in this book, I will make my case, if for no other reason at all than to get it off my chest. And who knows, it may even be the light that illuminates a path for you too to become a carpenter patriot. God only knows we need more.

> "It is curious that physical courage should be so common in the world, and moral courage so rare."   – Mark Twain

Bill Michel (1848-2010) was a close friend, a mentor, and one of Alaska's most talented bush pilots (portrait 1991). He started me down the road to becoming a carpenter patriot.

Immigration

"Listening to discussions of immigration laws and proposals
to reform them is like listening to something out of *Alice in
Wonderland*. Immigration laws are the only laws that are dis-
cussed in terms of how to help people who break them. One of
the big problems that those who are pushing 'comprehensive
immigration reform' want solved is how to help people who
came here illegally and are now "living in the shadows" as a
result. What about embezzlers or burglars who are 'living in
the shadows' in fear that someone will discover their crimes?
Why not 'reform' the laws against embezzlement or burglary
so that such people can also come out of the shadows? Almost
everyone seems to think that we need to solve the problem
of the children of illegal immigrants because these children
are here 'through no fault of their own.' Do people who say
that have any idea how many millions of children are living
in dire poverty in India, Africa, or other places 'through no
fault of their own' and would be better off living in the United
States? Do all children have some inherent right to live in
America if they have done nothing wrong? If not, then why
should the children of illegal immigrants have such a right?"
– Thomas Sowell (February 4, 2014 *National Review*)

THE USA FACES MANY important issues, but few draw so
much contention as immigration. The immigration debate may have
many facets nowadays, but it really all boils down to two foundational topics – the purpose of immigration to the USA and who
should be allowed to immigrate to the USA. It is these two topics that

7

I will discuss in a roundabout fashion. I believe they should be "no brainers" if someone knows anything about our country's founding doctrines, its Constitution, and its history.

I begin by saying that **Nowhere in the US Constitution does it say we are to have unbridled immigration or allow immigration that does not serve in the best interest of the country.** Inside the Statue of Liberty there is a plaque that says "Give me your tired, your poor, your huddled masses, yearning to breathe free, the wretched refuse of your teeming shore, send these, the homeless, tempest tossed to me, I lift my lamp beside the golden door." Does this single sentence pulled from a donated sonnet to help raise funds to build the statue's pedestal, delineate US immigration policy? Is that phrase saying that people from anywhere can flood into the USA illegally? Of course not. It speaks of America's rejection of the European feudalistic system and the "tired" being those held down and pushed around by it – the unprivileged. The Statue of Liberty was a belated gift from France in 1885 commemorating the alliance between her and the thirteen colonies during the American Revolution (some 109 years prior) and must be looked at in this light. The Revolutionary War was a fight for "Liberty" and thus the name of the statue. The statue faces out away from the USA and directs her hope of liberty to all the oppressed people in other nations of Europe. The Statue of "**Liberty**" has absolutely nothing to do with immigration other than that the boat loads of new immigrants passed by her on their way to be processed into the USA at Ellis Island. Lady Liberty originally came with only the date "July IV, MDCCLXXVI" (July 4, 1776) stamped on the statue's hand-held tablet. The now famous Emma Lazarus poem was affixed inside the pedestal in the early 1900s. The poem spoke to the heart of the huge masses of people that had arrived to American shores between 1820 and 1920 from Europe. During that time, the USA absorbed some 60% of the world's immigrants or over

30 million people (www.infoplease.com). The reason – an expanding nation needed cheap labor for its budding industries and settlers to populate its vast empty continent. *"A large population is a king's glory, but without subjects a prince is ruined"* (*Proverbs* 14:28). At some point in time, a drinking glass is full and you stop pouring in the liquid beverage. On that note, immigration policies began soon after the Statue of Liberty was erected and have continued ever since. Starting about 1924 there was a 40-year gap where immigration was very limited to allow assimilation of the huge amount of earlier immigrants and to permit middle class wages to rise. The immigrants of the early times came to build this country and invested their lives and blood into that process. They all brought a skill whether it was baking, boat building, farming, carpentry, etc. The immigrants since the 1980s have come to reap the welfare benefits of a system that they had no part in building. The majority of them came with no skill of any type.

James Madison, one of this nation's founders, laid out the primary principle of US immigration. Its purpose was to create the upward growth of this country economically, morally, intellectually, and spiritually. *"Not merely to swell the catalogue of people. No, sir, it is to increase the wealth and strength of the community; and those who acquire the rights of citizenship, without adding to the strength or wealth of the community, are not the people we are in want of."* (*Annals of the Congress of the United States*, Volume 1. "History of Congress." pgs 1111–1112)

I am a firm believer that there are many folks who have been allowed to immigrate to the USA since the 1980s that should not be here. They don't square with the country's principles/values and bring nothing of benefit to the table. It is not some God-given right that everyone who wants to come live in the USA be allowed to do so. This is totally absurd. Immigration wasn't intended to be a tool of diversity, but the method to bring in the best and brightest workers to help grow the country. We have strayed a long way from immigration's original purpose.

Multiculturalism was never something our forefathers accepted. They envisioned a "melting pot" society where folks came from all over to form one nation. They believed in set borders, one language, a common culture, and the rule of law. Assimilating requires that one accept the new culture with all its facets as your own. It means the giving up of the culture from whence you came to be a part of a new and different culture. This is a far cry from what has gone on in recent times where people storm the border in total disregard for the laws of the country, form their own segregated communities, keep their native tongue, demand that their previous culture be respected, and burden society by financial irresponsibility. None of these are acceptable to the creation of "one people" (*E pluribus unum* – "out of many one", the motto of the USA) and should not be allowed.

> "In the first place, we should insist that if the immigrant who comes here in good faith becomes an American and assimilates himself to us, he shall be treated on an exact equality with everyone else, for it is an outrage to discriminate against any such man because of creed, or birthplace, or origin. But this is predicated upon the person's becoming in every facet an American, and nothing but an American...There can be no divided allegiance here. Any man who says he is an American, but something else also, isn't an American at all. We have room for but one flag, the American flag... We have room for but one language here, and that is the English language... and we have room for but one sole loyalty and that is a loyalty to the American people."
> – Theodore Roosevelt

If someone comes to the USA, it must be by following the rules formulated by the people of this land. The owners (citizens) by virtue of their representatives (Congress) are the ones who have determined if/how/when/why one can visit their house (USA). Everybody has a door to the house where they live and it is opened to allow folks in when they are invited. You control who, when, for what purpose, and how long they stay. If someone snuck into your house and started living there uninvited you would not be very happy. To do so would be trespassing and effect removal and punishment for not respecting the property rights of the owner. The same should hold true for someone who enters the USA without permission. For the government to not punish illegal entries would be the same as law enforcement saying that this unknown individual who snuck into your house and took up residence without your permission must be allowed to stay, and, on top of that, you must give them a spot at your dinner table and feed them. And if "by chance" this individual was pregnant when she snuck into your house, her engendered arrival must automatically become a part of your natural family who is now due all the inherent rights of your other "real" children. Oh, and by the way, this unwelcome "guest" can invite any member of their own family to come stay in your house as well, and you are required to care for them also. Surely you can see the absurdity illustrated in my example, yet this goes on daily in the USA. In 2016, according to the Federation for American Immigration Reform (FAIR), these uninvited "guests" (illegal aliens) cost the US taxpayers some $116 billion and this cost grows each year.

Aside from the need to be invited based on bringing something of value to the table (imagine a pot luck dinner), only those who fit your idea of a decent guest and share the same values should be invited. Folks who come from countries that have a similar democratic or democratically inclined society and whose culture aligns with ours would make good guests (things in common). Whereas people from countries who desire to take over our country and force their depraved culture and way of thinking upon us (sharia law), do not make good guests and should never be invited. These types of visitors do not come in the spirit of joining with you (assimilating) but rather in subjugating you (enslaving). In the case of Muslims immigrating to the USA – I am totally against it. And I say this despite having Muslim friends and working closely with them in a foreign country. I continue to pray that they and every Muslim will be able to escape from the mind control that is Islam. Just as oil and water cannot be combined, the difference between Muslim culture and Judea Christian–based Western culture is irreconcilable and will always be such. Muslims have been at war with Western civilization for thousands of years. Their Quran demands it. There are well over 100 verses requiring jihad (or "holy" war) against non-believers. It is an important part of their ideology (www.thereligion-ofpeace.com). No one can assimilate into a society they hate and want to destroy. Even Muslims themselves tell us this – so why do we still accept them as immigrants? This makes absolutely no sense at all. Islam cleric Bujar Hysa clearly states that Islam cannot coexist with Democracy. Others like Lebanese immigrant Brigitte Gabriel declare the same: *"A practicing Muslim who believes the word of the Quran to be the word of Allah … who goes to mosque and prays every Friday, who prays five times a day – this practicing Muslim, who believes in the teachings of the Quran, cannot be a loyal citizen of the United States."*

It is my opinion that Islam is the biggest reproach to freedom in the USA today. Not only is Islam a deceptive false religion but behind it hides a despotic fascist political system of government that uses terrorism (violence, murder, torture, and rape) to instill totalitarian control. *"Islam is not a religion of peace, it's a political theory of conquest that seeks domination by any means"* and *"the Quran (sharia) is basically the constitution"* – Ayaan Hirsi Ali (former Somali Muslim). This is the monumental problem with Islam that many people refuse to see and accept – Islam is a tyrannical form of government disguised as a religion. By this disguise they are able to trigger most people's "fairness gene" so they will even defend Islam by stating that "it's only a religion," when in truth it is a vile Trojan horse. Only a naive, insane, or idiotic person would allow someone into their house whose sworn duty is to destroy that household. We fought to keep the fascist Axis Power out of the USA in World War II, why would we now bow down and allow something infinitely worse to infiltrate our society. The economist and social philosopher Wilhelm Ropke, the first professor fired by the Nazis for his ideas, defined Communism as a "pseudo-Islam" because both it and Islam are based on the principal of conquest and total domination. Every orthodox Muslim must accept sharia law. This includes its provisions about warring against nonbelievers, with the ultimate goal of converting, killing, or enslaving every last non-Muslim on earth. It is the president's responsibility to protect the US people and its culture, not aid in its demise as President Obama did. You cannot vet people without looking at their ideology and only a fool would suggest otherwise.

> "I don't care whether you worship a stone, just don't stone me with it … we will not abridge our freedoms so as to not offend savages."   – Pamela Geller

I personally would like to see anyone who does not denounce sharia law sent packing – citizen or not. I call it seditious conspiracy (18 U.S.C. § 2384). Then again who knows if they will be telling the truth since they are permitted to use "Taqiyya" (lie) to deceive non-Muslims about Islam and their intentions. One 2015 poll showed 51% of the Muslims living in the USA preferred to have the choice of being governed according to sharia (Islamic law) as compared to US law. In another 2015 poll, the Pew Research Center found 60% of "Muslim-Americans" (an oxymoron if there ever was one) under 30 years old were more loyal to Islam than to the USA. Just because the parental immigrant generation may remain as moderates (believers but not practicing Muslims) during their lifetime is certainly no guarantee that their children will not radicalize and turn to jihad and terrorism in the name of Islam. It happens all too often (i.e., Ahmad Kharn Rahami, Omar Mateen). Islam is a cancer. And like cancer it will never just disappear if left untreated but rather metastasize throughout the whole body. The only way to stop cancer is to destroy the mutant cells or surgically remove them. I will never forget September 11, 2001 where 2,977 people were viciously killed and over 6,000 injured at the hands of 19 Islamic terrorists. These 19 men were motivated to commit this atrocity by only one thing – their steadfast allegiance to Islam.

Some may say that I favor instilling a religious litmus test to enter the USA and that this is contra the First Amendment of the Constitution. I would argue they are taking this amendment way out of context. First, as I mentioned earlier, Islam is not a religion in the sense of the word but a fascist government system. Second, this amendment has nothing whatsoever to do with defining who can or cannot enter the USA. That is up to the people (Congress) to determine. *"Due process does not invest any alien with a right to enter the United States, nor confer on those admitted the right to remain against the national will. Nothing in the Constitution requires admission or sufferance of aliens hostile to our scheme of government."* – Justice Robert Jackson in Shaughnessy *v.* United States (1953). It is prudent thinking to restrict sworn enemies from infiltrating your country. The countries that do not accept Muslims, like Poland and Japan, have no terrorism. It is not hateful to want to protect one's homeland. The First Amendment states that "Congress shall make no law respecting an establishment of religion, or prohibiting the free exercise thereof." Keep it in context and it is very clear. This amendment was to bar a young America from ever following the path of England who had set a state-sanctioned religion. It was designed to dissuade problems between the Protestants and the Anglicans of that day. The Amendment is only applicable to how US **citizens** inside our borders are governed. It has absolutely nothing to do with folks who are not citizens outside our borders. It certainly was never intended to provide cover for an enemy to invade our land or be used as a justification to ethically and religiously transform the USA. Rather, it was intended to stop both of these abuses from happening, not augment them. Only a blind man can't see what is going on. Early immigrants like the pilgrims and others that followed shortly afterward came to "America" to escape religious persecution. This is the exact opposite of how the Muslims now come to the USA. They come from some 26 countries where Islam is the established mandated state religion, where clerics rule, and freedom of worship is not allowed. Their unabashed goal is to impose the same in all Western societies and openly claim they will use propagation and time as the method to accomplish it (*Stealth Invasion: Muslim Conquest through Immigration and Resettlement Jihad* – Leo Hohmann). If you try to immigrate to their countries as a Christian, the welcome you receive will be your end (YouTube: *Something to think about* – Steve Gern).

"The world is not ruined by the wickedness of the wicked, but by the weakness of the good." – Napoleon

Anyone who has worked in construction since the early 1990s has undoubtedly worked with Latinos. When I first entered construction in the early 1970s, the Vietnam War was winding down and the trades were dominated by Caucasian veterans. It was the only game in town. Sure, it was hard work, but if you wanted to eat, you worked. In the 1980s, we saw a large number of workers depart the trades for age-related reasons, and with the blossoming computer industry offering guys an alternative to the hot sweaty labor of construction work, many guys coming of work age in that decade chose an IT career over construction. Latinos took advantage of the worker shortfall and entered the building market in droves. They all had no training but quickly picked up the skills needed to work in a production era where more and more of the industry was turning toward prefabrication (trusses, etc.). A high percentage of these workers were illegal. They came from Mexico and Central America. They worked for cash as day laborers or picked up some type of false documents allowing them to be hired on the books. Many times it was with a borrowed Social Security Number that was shared between many, or they could buy a fake green card for as little as $100. The Mexican embassy was more than happy to help them skirt the US immigration laws. I worked with many of these guys while running other people's crews and grew to love them like family. I taught them as much as they could absorb and together we formed tight framing crews. Most came to the USA with the intent to make some money and send it back to their wife and kids, but quite often, within a few years, they had started a second family in the USA and their first family back at home was left to fend for themselves. Not only was it expensive to travel back to their home country, but they risked not being able to get back into the USA on their return so they didn't even try. Outside the border areas there are few to no immigration officers, so rarely did they have any problems. With a state-issued driver's license or ID they were just like a local. Some were able to sneak their wives into the states and that was soon followed by an anchor baby to end any deportation fears. Others, as mentioned, quickly married US citizens to negate the threat. Next, in both situations, one sees their extended family from home arriving by chain immigration. While I sympathize with these folks, many who are very dear friends, I cannot agree with their disregard and abuse of the approved entry and immigration system set up by the American people. Anchor babies and chain immigration should not be allowed – folks must stop twisting the Constitutional mandate out of context. Of the one million **legal** immigrants currently allowed into the USA per year (an amount equal to the entire population of Montana), 60 to 70% arrive via chain immigration (www.cis.org). Of that one million yearly amount, 14 in 15 supposedly come for other than work-related reasons (family unification), yet most all end up competing with citizens for jobs. Chain immigration has become the standard procedure for an unqualified individual to bypass the US immigration system's requirements of possessing a marketable skill and showing earning capability. During the past 50 years, over 36 million immigrants have entered the USA in this exploitative manner

Another huge problem for the USA along this line is the out-of-control influx of refugees. Without delving again into the utter stupidity of accepting folks as refugees who have nothing in common with our culture and won't assimilate, we need to limit the amount of refugees to a small number and then only for a short time. When the problem for which they fled their own country is resolved, they must go home. Accepting refugees should not be treated as an auxiliary method of immigration for folks who have nothing to offer our country and will only stay on welfare rather than work. The same exact thing holds true about this insanity of giving illegal immigrants amnesty. Not only is it plain wrong to bless a lawbreaker, but a 2016 National Academy of Sciences report (The Economic and Fiscal Consequences of Immigration) determined the net cost to be over $3.75 trillion if amnesty is enacted for the 10 million illegals currently in the USA. But even this astronomical expense doesn't begin to touch the injustice played on rightful US citizens who can't find a job as a result of this charade or the other legal immigrant applicants who have had to navigate a long and arduous process and are still waiting in line to be admitted. Ronald Reagan started this whole mess by giving amnesty to 2.7 million illegal immigrants in 1986. That number eventually mushroomed exponentially as a result of the chain migration rules of 1965. If he had not done that then, we would not be where we are today. Now this mockery of the people's legally approved system of immigration has been duplicated by the following presidents granting amnesty six more times. Amnesty, as a method to bypass the legal immigration system of the USA, is now firmly entrenched in the minds of everyone in the world. It has become a way to bring in your entire community. Amnesty is just the first wave. I have illegal friends who have shared this methodology with me – just sneak in, wait 5 to 6 years until amnesty is offered, and then go get the whole extended family. Amnesty is the immigration method used by those who can't make it into this country on their own merits and have no skills.

I have no problem with legal immigration if the economy is growing at such a rate that more new jobs are being created than can be filled internally by the work-age kids of current citizens entering the job market. This was the main intent of immigration from the Founders' days – to fill the shortfall with high-quality educated individuals. When the drinking glass is of a larger size, you can fit in more beverage (refers back to my earlier comment). Immigration should be contingent on the USA's economic condition not some magic number pulled out of thin air as in the current day policy.

Let's take a look at some immigration and jobs statistics for 2016 to see how poorly our current immigration is managed. To begin, most economists believe that the amount of new wage earners entering the US job market by internal population growth in 2016 was between 150,000 and 185,000 individuals a month (in the 1990s and 2000s it was up at +200,000). When the folks who have left the job market as a result of retirement or other reasons (58,000 per month) is subtracted from these numbers, we end up with an estimated net job need of between 92,000 and 127,000 new jobs per month. The US Bureau of Labor Statistics showed that job growth in 2016 averaged 186,000 new jobs created per month (www.bls. gov). On the surface, there appears to be more than enough new jobs produced to handle the new internal wage earners entering the job market that year, but before we can actually determine this, we must take into account three modifiers. The first modifier is that in 2007 to 2009, the USA suffered a major recession and 8.7 million jobs were lost from the economy. It took the following 5 to 6 years, or until the end of 2014, for job growth to regain those lost jobs alone. Now consider that from the start of the recession in 2007 until the end of 2014 (when the 8.7 million lost jobs were finally regained), new wage earners continued to enter the job market by internal population growth at between 150,000 and 185,000 per month with a net need for new jobs of 92,000 to 127,000 after the folks exiting the job market were taken into account. This normal growth went unanswered because the economy was fully engaged in just gaining back the 8.7 million lost jobs, and, thus, a pent-up demand of some 7.7 million folks needing jobs was created by the end of 2014 (conservative estimate: 92,000 × 84 months = 7.7 million). From 2015 and on, **any extra** job creation in the economy began going toward these 7.7 million unemployed folks. Depending on the condition of the economy, this could take about 8 years (until 2022) to zero out. Spreading this 7.7 million out over 8 years would require an additional 80,000 new jobs produced each month above and beyond the regular 92,000 to 127,000 that are needed to handle normal internal population growth (80,000 = 7.7 million/96 months). Now, as a second modifier, we must consider that **each year** the USA accepts as part of its immigration policy three groups of individuals: 1 million immigrants (stated earlier, www.dhs.gov); +700,000 guest worker visas for skilled and unskilled foreigners with their spouses (www.cis. org); and 85,000 refugees (www.migrationpolicy.org [year 2016]). These three groups combined could add as many as an additional 149,000 individuals per month to the new wage earners entering the job market category depending on how many are minors (149,000 = 83,300 new immigrants [1 million/12 months] + 58,300 work visas [700,000/12] + 7,000 refugees [85,000/12]). With the US economy just about level creating jobs for the 7.7 million unemployed folks, it now gets hit again by our dear US immigration system dumping up to an additional 149,000 job-needy individuals per month into the economy. And I must note that this migratory dumping of new individuals into the economy did not just happen for the year 2016 but is an ongoing policy that persists whether we are in a great recession/ recovery or not. Since we are working with rough numbers, I won't even include any extra pent-up demand caused by this absurd influx into my calculations but rather swap it for the minors that may be buried in the 1.085 million per year new immigrant and refugee categories. So, somehow the US economy, which is producing 186,000 jobs per month, is supposed to satisfy the need of between 321,000 and 356,000 individuals entering the work marketplace per month (321,000 to 356,000 = 92,000 to 127,000 internal growth + 80,000 to recuperate pent-up demand caused by recession + 149,000 imported laborers). Evidently, few of our bureaucrats in DC know how to use a calculator for I find that we had a shortfall of 135,000 to 171,000 created jobs per month in 2016. This alone is devastating, but it gets even worse when you consider as a third modifier that there were/are 50,000 illegals per month who sneak across the border or overstay tourist visas (www.pewhispanic.org), and +800,000 DACA (Deferred Action for Childhood Arrivals) illegals who are also vying for jobs. Looking at US historical jobs growth data, I found that only seldom has the number of new jobs produced in the US economy ventured into the +300,000 per month range with the best yearly job production average reaching close to the 250,000 per month range. In 2016, only 63% of potential US workers were actually working, and the labor participation rate was near a 38-year low (www.bls.gov). Therefore, 45,800,000 folks were left without jobs that year (123.8 million potential workers [2016] × 37% = 45.8 million). I doubt I need to say more.

What recent administrations have done with immigration is the same thing the Federal Reserve has done in expanding the money supply. By printing dollars through their idiotic QE (quantitative easing) policy rather than tying money supply increases to a percentage rise in the GDP (Gross Domestic Product), they have devalued the dollar (see the Money Supply section farther along). With immigration, the leftists are turning the USA into a Third World country – an overabundance of available labor and few jobs. They did/do it for both political (more leftist voters – 80% vote Democratic Party) and financial (low-cost labor for personal or corporate benefit) reasons. Because Third World countries suffer from corrupt misman-agement is certainly no reason to bring the same failures into the USA. An overabundance of labor is a spiral to hell. It only serves to drive a given wage down into the sewer, which then results in calls for raising the minimum wage so people can survive (basi-cally subsidize them), which then "of course" only serves to further destroy business efficiency, all the while condemning high-school age workers from achieving any success in finding work, so instead they go out and cause trouble. If the bureaucrats in charge would simply manage immigration correctly, there would never be a need to worry about wages. It all comes down to a simple economic supply and demand equation.

Therefore, allowable immigration amounts should be based on the unmet labor market's need above what is supplied by internal population growth. This amount is easy to know since the US Bureau of Labor Statistics publishes monthly job growth numbers. **Right now, general immigration should be stopped dead until such time that future payroll growth can repair the damage done by the federal government's irresponsible immigration disaster.** Who knows, but this may take several decades to bring wages back up to on par with an inflation-adjusted wage from the 1970s, which was before this insane immigration dumping began. Jobs should be for citizens first, and then, if we have additional needs, we can consider bringing in immigrants. The better the economy is growing the more folks can be allowed in as immigrants but not in an amount that will cause a downward pressure on a given wage. It is bad enough how socialistic regulation is killing production in the economy, but to dump new immigrants on top of a constricting economy is nothing short of moronic. It has been a disaster for many of us regular Americans. Over my lifetime, a dramatic loss in real wages has been thrust upon a carpenter as a result. In 1978, I earned $20 per hour as framing foreman for a Santa Barbara builder ($40,000 per year before taxes), which was about two-thirds of what a roof cutter or wall layout guy made as a piecemeal carpenter in the housing tracts a few years earlier. That same 1978 wage, when adjusted for inflation would be $78 per hour ($158,000 per year) in 2016 dollars (calculator.net). This straight line inflation adjustment would also be alleging that, since 1978, I never learned one more thing to increase my earning potential, which of course is totally absurd. Sad to say, but in 2016, if I wasn't disabled, I would be lucky to make $25 per hour ($50,000 per year) **or approximately 32% of the value of my 1978 wage** on a straight line adjustment. If one estimates that over my +40-year career I might have doubled my earning potential in real terms due to an increase in knowledge then my $25 per hour wage today would be less than 20% of the value of my 1978 wage. While it is true that the development of labor-saving equipment (pneumatic nailers, telehandlers, etc.) and some increased application of prefabricated materials to custom home building may have had a slight dampening effect on wage growth, the overlying reason for the drastic fall in my wages and those of other manual workers in construction has been irrational immigration – **both legal and illegal** – creating an oversupply of workers. This glut of workers when combined with poor economic growth as a result of government overregulation has caused wage stagnation spanning over three decades for non-union and union alike. How sad. You can now see how false the assumption that "illegals take jobs US citizens won't do" is. In reality the opposite is true. The reason citizens won't make careers in manual labor type jobs like rough carpentry anymore is because the use of illegal labor has lowered a given wage or any wage growth in that market so much that citizens must find other types of jobs where they can make a decent wage in order to support their families. Carpentry used to be a good career choice – not any more.

Data shows that some 5 million jobs in the manufacturing industries were sent overseas during the 2000s. In recent years, the USA has lost over 70,000 factories and a third of all these types of jobs nationwide. While it is true that a few of these jobs may have been lost to technological advances, most were lost as the result of absurd US government regulation that simply drove these companies out of business. The few remaining ones that regulation did not kill headed out of town to escape ridiculously high corporate taxes. Good evidence that we have folks with absolutely no concept of economic principles running the government and/or are intent on sacrificing the mostly white middle class working man and the family structure to globalization. The only folks who have stayed well ahead of inflation are government workers and lawyers. This doesn't surprise me at all, just more despairing evidence of how little the oligarchy cares what happens to us regular folk. So not only are we allowing immigrants to come in and take over our US jobs, but we are also sending the few remaining jobs overseas so the other family members of the immigrant's family who didn't make it in by chain immigration can have a job.

> "Nothing has done more to undermine our sense of common responsibility than our failed welfare system. ... It rewards welfare over work. ... We have to make welfare what it was meant to be, a second chance, not a way of life."
> – Bill Clinton (1995 State of the Union)

As a sidebar to the subject on immigration I would note that the government's welfare safety net needs to be dissolved immediately, especially for immigrants. Although the Personal Responsibility and Work Opportunity Reconciliation Act of 1996 declares immigrants "not eligible for any Federal means-tested public benefit for a period of 5 years beginning on the date of the alien's entry," this law is rarely enforced. Statistics show that an inordinately high amount of all immigrants depend on the welfare system to survive. Some 90% of all Muslim immigrants are on the take (Office of Refugee Resettlement statistics – ORR) and 68% of all Muslims want bigger government and more services (PEW Research). The average federal welfare benefits of immigrant-headed households, legal or illegal, was $6,234 in 2012 according to the Center for Immigration Studies. These high numbers demonstrate not only the sheer failure of the US immigration policy, but also the absolute fiasco that is the socialist's welfare state. I believe welfare should be a privately based charity affair. If no help can be found from the individual's own extended family, then a church or other group can step in to help. If a new immigrant can't make it here by the sweat of his own brow as the many generations before him have done (in much more trying situations) without welfare, then he/she should go home. I see welfare as nothing more than the legalized theft from one group of people who are leading a responsible life to be transferred to others who are not. Consider the growth in food stamps (SNAP): In 2016 some $71 billion was spent on this "hand out" as compared with just $18 billion in 2000. A society should not be overloaded with folks who do not want to pull their own weight. Granted, many folks become disabled or hurt in the process of work or life, but there are other specific programs designed to help them. Welfare is a huge incentive for an individual to be a lazy bum or provides the free time to immerse oneself in things like terrorism, gang violence, etc. My wife, to satisfy her own curiosity on how the welfare system works in the USA, went undercover in Oakland, CA, and was absolutely horrified by the rampant abuse of the system. *"If a man doesn't want to work, he shouldn't eat"* (2 *Thessalonians* 3:10). *"A worker's appetite works for him, For his hunger urges him on"* (*Proverbs* 16:26).

Bear in mind that my comments on immigration come not only from common sense and study, but also from my personal experience immigrating (gaining residency) to a "Third World country" for humanitarian aid purposes. I have a unique window into the immigrant's strife that only foreign missionaries can share. As a result, I have been exposed to conditions that are so far below the poverty level of the USA that it makes you cry. "I do understand" – I have lived it. To gain residency, I followed the applicable immigration laws, learned to speak the language, and adapted to the culture and its norms. Many people in the USA feel that it is unkind to round up illegals and throw them out. Well, let me tell you that if you are found to have entered illegally into any of the countries in Central and South America you will pay dearly, and your chance to reenter at a future date after being thrown out is near zilch. Other nations are serious about their laws and they enforce them firmly, as they should. Additionally some folks in the USA bitch about a proposed requirement that one must have a state-issued ID to vote. Well, where I have lived, if you can't show your official ID to any government official when he asks, off to the local jail you go. Even the poorest of the poor must have their national identity card. It has a photo, signature, and thumb print so it cannot be stolen like happens in the USA with our Social Security Numbers. This ID is of one type for citizens and of a totally different type for anyone else. A noncitizen's ID clearly shows their current migratory status along with its expiration date. Surprise road blocks are frequently set up to check IDs. None of this bothers me, and I personally believe it is acting responsibly and certainly serves as a deterrent for illegal immigration and crime. The people of a country have the sovereign right to dictate the terms by which anyone is allowed into their country either for a visit or permanently. It is their country after all. If you get caught as an illegal immigrant in Mexico you are automatically convicted of a crime equivalent to a US felony and spend 2 years in jail. Get caught in the country illegally a second time, you spend 10 years in that same sleazy jail cell.

Folks who are in the USA illegally do not have the rights afforded to citizens or legal visitors by the US Constitution and none should be provided them. It is a known crime to enter our country illegally or overstay your visitor's visa. When caught, these folks should either pay a fine and be deported or spend time in jail and be deported. No court proceedings. Everything they have materially gained during their illegal stay in the USA should be confiscated. Breaking the immigration law should have this penalty, period. An illegal or legal resident who has no right to vote but registers and votes anyway should be severely punished. There is no excuse whatsoever – it is pure seditious conspiracy. The court system is in place to defend the rights of citizens and folks who are here legally. This lunacy of giving illegals undeserved "due process of law" rights in the USA system is costing the American taxpayers billions of dollars and must stop. People who sneak into the USA all know it is a crime, but they do it anyway – they have seen over many decades that the US government has no spine to enforce its own laws.

> "More fundamentally, why do the American people not have a right to the protection that immigration laws provide people in other countries around the world – including Mexico, where illegal immigrants from other countries do not get the special treatment that Mexico and its American supporters are demanding for illegal immigrants in the United States?"
> – Thomas Sowell (February 4, 2014 *National Review*).

I also know the frustration of trying to immigrate to another country and being rejected. In 1993, I tried to immigrate to Australia to teach rough carpentry. Following my back injury in 1987 with its resulting disability, this seemed like a reasonable consideration, since Australia was crying out for building instructors, and only jobsite experience was required. I had previously attended an Outward Bound course in Australia's Smokey Mountains and, as a result, had fallen in love with the country and the people. My Australian classmates were the ones who suggested that I immigrate; they really wanted me to come. Anyhow, despite being the author of a construction manual and quite skilled in my craft I was rejected because my carpentry training had been acquired outside the carpenters' union. My hefty application fee went down the drain. Australia did modify their immigration rules a few years later, making it more favorable to my situation, but by then it was too late for me since to get in the door as a tradesman I had to be younger than 40 years.

I believe our forefathers had a society in mind where everyone was given the same opportunity to succeed. There was to be no preferential treatment. It was up to you whether you succeeded or not. Equal outcomes as is now mandated by the federal government (things like affirmative action, etc.) was the farthest thing from our forefather's minds.

I was a young man when the USA was facing the racial strife of the 1960s but knew little of what was going on. We didn't get the newspaper and only listened to the radio when the president was going to address the nation on some matter. I personally was so swamped with my chores on the farm and studying to do well in school that, even if we did get a newspaper, I doubt I would have taken time to glance at it. I grew up color blind and just figured everyone else did as well. To me, some of us just had more or less melanin in our skin – that's all. I have spent a good deal of time in Belize over the years as a humanitarian aid volunteer. While the hot humid climate is not one of my favorites, I absolutely love the people. I believe the Belizean society is more in line with what our forefathers had in mind. Certainly not the big mess we now have in the USA, where everybody has to say whether they are "African-American" or "Chinese-American" or "Mexican-American", etc. To me it shows that they have an allegiance to some other country. *"A house divided against itself cannot stand"* (taken from *Mark* 3:25) was used by Abraham Lincoln in an address in 1858 regarding the North and South split over secession and slavery. It has once again become applicable to the USA, but from a different standpoint. I see all these folks spouting "xxx-American" jargon as false jingoists, because not one of them would return to live in their ancestral lands even if you paid them a million bucks to do so. You will never hear this kind of blabber in Belize. Belizeans have no allegiance to any other part of the world, only Belize. "I am Belizean" comes through loud and clear. They are fiercely patriotic. You could be white, black, brown, yellow, red, green, or purple but "we are all Belizeans." They do not talk colors or races. You will not hear "he is white" or "she was black" or "he was Chinese," etc., in Belize. On your ID it simply says "light complexion, medium complexion, or dark complexion." No one's ancestry has anything to do with it. Belize is a successful example of our forefather's "melting pot" idea. We need to implement this model. No more "xxx-American," it is time to decide on your allegiance. Let's use myself as an example. I am a mutt. I have a little bit of everything in my blood from Scotch-Irish to Swedish to Czechoslovakian to Creek Indian, and only God knows what else. I don't look at the countries where my historical bloodline originated as having anything to do with me here and now. I have never visited those countries, nor is it likely that I ever will. I have zero allegiance to them. The "Holladays" immigrated here in the 18th century and from that time forward my bloodline is "American," plain and simple. Just because I have a taste of American Indian in my blood does not make me any more American than anyone else. How I got here is unimportant, but what I do while here is. I am blessed to be here and so is every other American of any complexion.

> "The idea of 'hyphenated Americanism' is a trick of the cultural-Marxists intended to divide America against itself for the purposes of weakening our autonomy and anesthetizing us to globalism."   – Mychal Massie

Social Security

FDR WOVE SOCIALISM INTO the national fabric starting with the introduction of the Social Security Act in 1935. This was followed in 1965 by LBJ with Medicare and Medicaid, and 2010 with the Affordable Care Act by Obama. There are also various other welfare programs designed to transfer money from the producers in America to the nonproducers. These programs have weakened the country's work ethic, developed friction between the various income levels, and destroyed our culture. Personally, I believe the legalized Ponzi scheme of Social Security should be shut down immediately and the money that folks have paid into the system should be returned with interest. What kind of financial sense does it make to have someone who may have paid a total of $50,000 into Social Security over their 25- to 30-year work history be given a return of $500,000 during the following 25 years of retirement. When you add in the benefits paid out for medical treatment (some of which are astronomically expensive) by Medicare, it is obvious that someone else has had to make some hefty financial outlays to supplement the program. We are talking about future generations paying for a debt they had no part in accumulating. Social Security perpetuates irresponsibility and is nothing more than legalized theft from a future generation to give to the current one (how about taxation without representation). Rather than acting responsibly and planning for the future, folks now depend on this robbery so they can survive when

31

retired. I have seen cases where folks spend their savings on elaborate vacations while setting nothing aside for the future, knowing they will have SS to live on when they "retire." Their "vacations" in this case are paid for by future taxpayers. What a shame! Where did this "retirement" stuff come from in the first place? You don't see it in the Bible or the lives of our forefathers. If you have been financially successful in this life, that's great – you will have more capacity to give back to society as you slowdown in your elder years. But to just go out and golf or fish 25 years away smacks of a hedonistic view of life.

Congress, the President,
and the Supreme Court

"It is hard to imagine a more stupid or more dangerous way
of making decisions than by putting those decisions in the
hands of people who pay no price for being wrong."
                                                    – Thomas Sowell

MOST OF US ARE pretty disgusted with the elitist Congress
and that is to say nothing of the imperial president that Obama was.
The House of Representatives (HR) was designed to represent us
common folks, it is our greatest voice. The brief 2-year term kept
each representative on a short leash and dependent on his constit-
uents. "*A government by representatives elected by the people at
short periods was our object, and our maxim...*" – Thomas Jefferson
to Samuel Adams (1800). The founders also felt that having new
blood cycle through the governing system was healthy and bene-
ficial in many ways. "*Whenever a man has cast a longing eye on
[offices] a rottenness begins in his conduct.*" – Thomas Jefferson to
Tench Coxe (1799). Seems like this ideal went by the wayside, for
today we have folks who have been in the HR for 40 to 50 yrs. How
can they possibly know anything about the lives of the regular folks
whom they purportedly represent. Few have ever even held a "real"
job in the economy of their district. Most are continually reelected
solely because of party affiliation and name recognition, not by merit.

By allowing these "professional" politicians to run the government, we have created an elitist ruling class – the exact opposite of the Constitution's intent and the example given by our forefathers who were all working folks at different levels. Nowadays, Washington, DC is filled with intellectuals who are idiots. Few are even capable of doing simple everyday household tasks that the rest of us must do just to live. I believe we need to change the Constitutional eligibility requirements for a position in the HR or the executive branch, that it only be open to folks who have worked a "real" job in the private sector where they desire to represent for a minimum of 5 years. By a "real" job, I mean some type of work that actually produces an economic product or service that contributes to the nation's GDP instead of detracting from it – certainly not a lawyer, a government employee, a pro athlete, a college professor, a reporter, an entertainer, or a community organizer, etc. I am not saying these folks don't work, they certainly do, and many quite hard, but they play no true role in the advancement of our "engine room" economy. The world of these folks is like another planet when compared to the world where most Americans live. Back in the early days of our country, all the players started off as youngsters working "real" jobs where they got their hands dirty, whether it be as a farm laborer, a seamstress, a printer, a sailor, a carpenter, etc., before ever becoming involved in politics, so they had real life experience to draw upon. This is the exact opposite of most of today's career politicians who live a life that is totally isolated from the results of the laws and regulations they create. Elitists like Barak Obama, John McCain, Joe Biden, Hillary Clinton, John Kerry, Bernie Saunders, Nancy Pelosi, among many others on both sides of the aisle, should have been required to spend some quality time living in "realsville" before pretending to represent us folks who actually do live there. Let's just look at one of these bozos for an example – Bernie Saunders. His resume shows that before he got his first long-term full-time job at 39 years old, which was a government job, he flipped around doing odd jobs, was a political activist and war protestor, and lived on public assistance. He tried carpentry very briefly but found it too difficult. Yeah, I would suppose so – the guy doesn't know how to work and prefers everybody else give him what he needs rather than apply himself. He is the perfect example of a genuine flake. Government handouts are all the guy knows whether it be welfare or "govfare" (welfare in the form of an exorbitantly overpaid government job) and understandably why he ended up as a loony Communist. He has absolutely zip in common with the everyday hard-working individual, only other losers like himself who want everything to be free. Our government is packed full of turkeys similar to him at many levels who couldn't or can't make it in the real world. Even a medical student must do a long arduous internship before he/she can start his/her practice as a full-fledged physician. Should we require anything less from our politicians. A simple 5-year stint as a normal person would certainly serve as a good internship. If they can't make it there, why would we want them to represent us. *"Select ... capable, honest men who fear God and hate bribes. Appoint them as leaders. ..."* (*Exodus* 18:21). Certainly, to graduate from an Ivy League school does show that you are able to sit through hours of listening to "crap" but does any university education ever help to develop one's critical thinking skills and problem solving ability or instill empathy and camaraderie toward the working man? Only living in "realsville" can do that.

Sometimes I wonder if we would be better served if the names of folks to represent an area where just pulled out of a hat instead of operating local elections to get a representative. I would love to see a better cross section of our society fill the peoples' house (HR), instead of just a bunch of lawyers. We should have plumbers, teachers, waitresses, secretaries, truck drivers, pilots, bakers, salesmen, loggers, fishermen, doctors, mechanics, barbers, and carpenters, etc.; all show up to do a stint in DC and then go back to their regular life. But does regular Joe the plumber have the time, money, and expertise to mount an election campaign? Of course not, yet he is the heart and soul of America. The folks who end up as our representatives in the HR nowadays are typically better off financially than most and have lots of business connections, wealthy friends, etc., that support their campaign (a rare exception would be someone like Sarah Palin). When these folks go to Washington, DC (DC), who do you think they represent? Doesn't take a genius to see through that one – of course it is the companies, wealthy folks, etc., who spent their bucks to get them elected. The regular folks come in third after their own personal ambitions to be reelected. Another problem I see is how external forces have been allowed to influence local elections. I do not believe anyone should be allowed to accept donations from outside their specific election district. If a candidate can't raise the funds to run from within his/her own district, then maybe they shouldn't be running. Term limits are a popular idea that many say will help cycle new blood through the HR more frequently. But I wonder if this will actually give a better voice to us regular folks or will it just make for a quicker turnover between self-serving elites?

> "Ask not what your country can do for you–ask what you can do for your country."
> – John Fitzgerald Kennedy (1961 Inaugural Address)

Maybe, if we returned to the original idea of a public "servant" where pay is more along the lines of doing jury duty service as opposed to receiving an insanely high wage with all kind of benefits, would we get rid of all the money-grubbing politicians. Some folks say that Congress is too complicated for the everyday Joe and for this reason we need professionals. Well, if that is true, then we need to simply things so they can be understood by everyday Joe. Doesn't the Constitution begin with the words *"We the people..."* and didn't Abraham Lincoln state that we have a *"government of the people, by the people, and for the people..."*? I can't find "by the professional politician" anywhere. A friend of mine once told me of a study that he had read about where a group of everyday Joes were pitted against a group of highly paid "experts" to see who made better overall decisions. I don't remember the specific details of how the test was performed, but I do recall that the everyday Joes won the match-up and made better choices. Doesn't really surprise me. *"If your mind is empty, it is always ready for anything, it is open to everything. In the beginner's mind there are many possibilities, in the expert's mind, there are few. That is the real secret of the arts, always be a beginner."* – Shunryu Suzuki

> "It will be of little avail to the people that the laws are made by men of their own choice if the laws be so voluminous that they cannot be read, or so incoherent that they cannot be understood."
>
> – James Madison

Whereas a representative in the HR was linked directly to the people in a particular district or area, a Senator was to be linked to a state as a whole. His responsibility was to represent his state's general interests in the Republic's government and served a longer 6-year term. As originally laid out in the US Constitution and Federalist 62/63, each state's legislature chose two individuals as their representatives. More than likely, these would be seasoned state government politicians. That format was changed in 1913 by the 17th Amendment to elect senators by public popular vote. Personally, I believe this change was a very bad idea and has done great damage to the function of the nation as a Republic. When a senator was chosen by the state's legislature his allegiance would naturally be to the state and its agenda or he would only see one term. As a result of now being elected by popular vote: his first allegiance would no longer be to his state, but to the companies, wealthy folks, etc., who financially supported his campaign for election; second comes his own personal ambitions of reelection, and third, the very last on his list are the people of his state. The exact same progression as the folks elected to the HR. This is exactly why we see so much "pork barrel" spending and crony capitalism. It's payback time when these corruptibles get to DC.

Congress needs to clean up its act; it is a real mess over there. Let's get serious about doing a job. Bills introduced in either house should just pertain to one subject matter alone. This procedure of tacking on "riders" needs to be eliminated entirely. Let's stop all the funny procedural games like senate filibustering to bar something from even getting to the floor for a vote. Let it have a simple up or down vote. Besides acting like a bunch of spoiled infants, Congress has already enacted so many blooming laws and regulations that one can rest assured that, at any moment, you are in violation of something. Our system of law began as a copy of British Common Law and was so impeccably simple. It followed two principles: Do all you say you are going to do (contract law), and don't do anything that will be a bother to your neighbor (civil law). This simplicity has mushroomed into a freaking nightmare (*Code of Federal Regulations* 175,500 pages in 2013). I would like to see us go back to Ronald Reagan's modus operandi that called for every new regulation/law to be enacted be accompanied by two regulations/laws that are to be rescinded. It is the only way to bring some sanity back.

I don't think I need to say anything about the Imperial presidency (2009–2017) which wandered so far from the Constitutional mandate that it is nearly unrecognizable. We need to elect presidents who love our country as originally formed and therefore will follow through on their vows to "uphold the Constitution of the USA" instead of trying to instill their father's anti-American dream (*The Roots of Obama's Rage* – Dinesh D'Souza). This BS of using "Executive Orders," as a method to negate laws passed by Congress or make an end run around Congress and create law when you don't get your way (i.e., Obama and DACA) must stop. Executive orders are the means by which the executive branch directs enforcement of the laws passed by Congress not a means to castrate them. The presidency as operated during the Obama administration showed a total disrespect for the people and the US Constitution. Basically, they used the system to ram a socialist globalist agenda down peoples' throats. Of course, this stems from their elitist mentality that believes all us regular folks are idiots, so they must implement what is best for us in spite of the Constitution and our objections. It is high time to stop presidential abuse of power. The people (Congress) need to quickly slap down Executive Orders that stray outside their intended Constitutional purpose of enforcing law. But, of course, to get a Congress that will fight for the people and follow the Constitution presents its own difficulties. The early presidents hardly ever used Executive Orders because the central government was small and nonintrusive, whereas these new-age, big-government presidents from Theodore Roosevelt on forward use it on a weekly basis to meddle in nearly every aspect of our lives.

The president has **no** authority to make treaties with other nations without the advice from and two-thirds approval of the Senate. If any piece of paper represents a "contract/agreement" between the USA and another country/countries/council/whatever on any subject, it is a treaty no matter what the executive branch wants to call it, and therefore must be approved by the state's representatives. This would make something like the Paris Climate agreement, which President Obama singularly arranged, totally illegal and shows a major abuse of power. It should never be about what the president or any administrator wants, but rather what the people (stock holders) want. The people are the ones who will be affected and will have to shoulder the cost of anything, whether it be some type of international accord or a change in immigration policy, so they rightfully control the reins. The president should oversee the executive branch similarly to how a CEO oversees a commercial company. He has been assigned the responsibility of enforcing the instructions and mandates given him by the people whether he agrees with them or not. He cannot choose what laws he will or will not enforce. If the president is recalcitrant to do his job, he should be thrown out or resign and replaced by someone who will do the job.

> "If in the opinion of the People, the distribution or modification of the Constitutional powers be in any particular wrong, let it be corrected by an amendment in the way which the Constitution designates. But let there be no change by usurpation; for though this, in one instance, may be the instrument of good, it is the customary weapon by which free governments are destroyed."   – George Washington

The scope of the presidency is all laid out in the Constitution, but as we all could see during the Obama administration, without a Congress that has any "balls" to keep the president in line or even own up to their own responsibilities (i.e., no trade promotion authority (TPA) "fast track" type authority should ever be granted), it will only be adhered to if the person in this leadership role is an individual of true character. Does a person of character fly himself and his family all over the globe taking extravagant vacations on the taxpayer's dime when the regular guy in the trenches is having a hard time just putting bread on the table and the country he represents is $20 trillion in debt (Barack Obama)? Does a first lady really need 24 assistants (Michelle Obama)? What kind of example is this? The total annual cost to support the Obama White House was $1.4 billion and this doesn't include executive policy operations only household costs (*The 1.4 Billion Dollar Man: Costs of the Obama White House* – Michael Groom). Other presidents have been nearly as lavish. Pretty sad. Congress should place a cap on the costs that we the taxpayers will pay for presidential household expenses and travel. The president must be held responsible to work within a reasonable budget just like we normal folks must. According to Michael Groom, "the British royal family received less than $50 million in taxpayer funds in 2011, an amount that would have kept the Obama White House running for about nine days." Truly amazing!

Another thing that has to go are these administrative agencies (EPA, FCC, FWS, FTC, HHS, ICC, NLRB, OSHA, etc.). They are totally outside the Constitutional control of the people. These agencies have the power to legislate, execute, and adjudicate – all three of the powers of the federal government wrapped up in one cute little package. They operate with total immunity and are not elected by the people. How did this all come about? How did they gain a "kingship" over some particular part of the American economy. Once again, this trash was introduced by early progressive presidents (Theodore Roosevelt and Woodrow Wilson) in order to expand the federal government's ability to control more aspects of citizen's lives. It has now been amplified to its current "untouchable" status by successive administrations on both sides of the aisle in their greed for power. The use of administrative agencies was the method specifically devised to covertly pull power out of the hands of the people (Congress) and give it to a group of so called "experts" because they supposedly know better. Really? They have succeeded in putting the America people back in the pre–Revolutionary War bondage. I have no problem with Congress consulting a group of experts on an area of policy, but their input should be just that – "**input**" – and nothing more. Congress (the people's reps) is the only part of the government conscripted by the Constitution with the task of making laws, and they cannot delegate this power and authority to anyone else. Same holds true of the Executive and Judicial branches – they cannot delegate their power and responsibilities to others. This transformation from a Constitutional Government to an Administrative State has gone on over the past 100 years and was all done without changing the Constitution via amendment as is required. The US Constitution limited the federal government's control over citizens' lives to a relatively small number of items, everything else not specifically listed was to be dealt with at the local level (state, county, city) where normal folks could best handle it for their particular situation. But, unfortunately, the federal government, being a power-hungry monster, has now forced itself into areas where it should never be. (Heritage Foundation: *From Administrative State to Constitutional Government*)

And while we are on the subject of unaccountability, we need to bring up the third branch of the government, this joke of a Supreme Court. It, like the executive branch, has decided that they too want in on the fun of making laws. The Constitution be damned, for it is not even referred to anymore when the Court is in session, only former misapplied decisions. Without even hiding their intention, activist judges do what they can to advance the Democratic Party's socialist globalist agenda. They are nothing more than political hacks. I was sorely disappointed back in 1987 when the nomination of Judge Robert Bork, one of this century's most brilliant legal minds, went unapproved. Personally, I believe the terms of the Justices of the Supreme Court should be limited to maybe 8 to 10 years and that Congress should be able to overrule their decisions with a two-thirds majority vote. The founders felt the same as Alexander Hamilton voiced in Federalist No. 78: "*The Constitution ought to be preferred to the statute, the intention of the people to the intention of their agents. Not does this conclusion by any means suppose a superiority of the judicial to the legislative power. It only supposes that the power of the people is superior to both; and that where the will of the legislature, declared in its statutes, stands in opposition to that of the people, declared in the Constitution, the judges ought to be governed by the latter rather than the former.*" Mark Levin did an excellent expose on how the Supreme Court has slid away from its Constitutional mandate in *Men in Black: How the Supreme Court Is Destroying America* and is definitely worth a read.

To finish up this topic on "Congress, the President, and the Supreme Court," I want to share that, in my opinion, no way should any Muslim who is already a citizen of the USA ever be allowed to hold any legislative, executive, or judicial government position – period. Since Muslims cannot truthfully pledge undivided allegiance to the USA they have no place in government. While the scripture *"No one can serve two masters. Either you will hate the one and love the other, or you will be devoted to the one and despise the other"* (*Matthew* 6:24) refers to trying to serve both God and money, its principle easily illustrates the reason for my objection. Muslims cannot be afforded any further opportunities to implement their sharia law agenda and change our country from its foundational principles. *"A little yeast works through the whole batch of dough."* (*Galatians* 5:9) Of course, many may say that my suggestion goes against Article 6 of the Constitution in regard to a religion test being used as a deterrent from holding public office, to which I would respond, as I already did in the immigration section earlier, that Islam is not a religion but an invading political force and therefore restrictions can easily be set as was done after World War II to combat the Communist party's influence (The Internal Security Act of 1950).

Taxes

THE CITIZENS AND BUSINESSES of the USA paid over $6 trillion dollars in federal, state, and local taxes in 2017. That is more than the GDP of all but a few countries of the world. Total insanity! While we suffer from taxes ad infinitum, the one I find the most grating is income tax. While Congress definitely has the power to levy taxes, a strong case can be made that the founders felt a man's labor was to be exempted from direct government taxation. Their belief was that import tariffs and excise tax (i.e., consumption type tax) should serve as the primary source of government revenue. This policy lasted through the first 137 years of our country's existence. I can still recall the good old days in the 1970s when construction workers were frequently paid in green dollar bills each Friday afternoon. You got your whole pay, not some dinky amount that remained after the government got done sucking your check dry. I wish it was still this way, because I have always disliked being forced to pay income taxes on hard labor. Tax unearned income if you must, but not a man's sweat labor. The 16th Amendment which gave the government power to tax income without apportionment was ratified in 1913. It was part of the progressive's income redistribution scheme and has done much to disincentive earnings through work. I would love to see the 16th Amendment repealed, but that is unlikely, in which case, an across-the-board flat rate income tax above a set personal exemption is the most fair. We must stop soaking the wealthy folks because of class envy. They are the ones who grow the private sector (GDP) by investing in products, projects, and innovation. Since politicians are always raising rates, I would like to see this flat tax rate set in stone so it is unchangeable. If this needs to be done through a Constitutional Amendment, then so be it, but I am tired of these bozos in Congress constantly jerking the rate upward. Per capita taxes have more than doubled since JFK (1961–1963). I believe that calculating and collecting this flat tax should be done in such a simple manner that the Internal Revenue Service can be disbanded, and their employees together with all the private tax preparers will now have the grand opportunity to get "real" jobs. OK, you are right, they may have to keep a couple people around to look over everybody's one-page computerized tax return. Corporate taxes should go bye-bye since it is nothing more than double taxation. The profit is already taxed once on their shareholders tax returns. One thing is for sure, a flat rate income tax would finally put an end to tax loopholes, special deductions, etc. They either subsidize certain groups (like home owners), spurn crony capitalism (wind power companies, electric car companies, etc.), or subsidize leftist states (state tax deductions from federal filing).

Voting

VOTING HAS ALWAYS BEEN an important **privilege** of American citizens, but over my lifetime it has become so degraded by the leftists. They will do almost anything to stay in power so they can extend and enlarge their socialist redistribution agenda. Their biggest play is unfettered open immigration to gain new democratic voters. They fail to enforce immigration statutes and openly accept any and all who make it over the line. Once here, there is that grand prize of welfare benefits (food, housing, medical, telephone) waiting courtesy of the hard-working American. Leftists strive to lower the citizenship requirements so it is faster and easier for aliens to vote (for them). Illegal immigrants head for the left-leaning big city states (California, Texas, Florida, New York, and Washington) where census apportionment allows these invaded states to unconstitutionally gain additional members in the HR and rob the citizen-voters in other states (Indiana, Iowa, Mississippi, Montana, North Carolina, Ohio, Oklahoma, and Pennsylvania) of their rightful representation. The inflated counts also affect the presidential election by increasing the number of votes some states get in the Electoral College. Leftists care little for the Constitution or the nation they are destroying. In their mind, it was illegitimate from the start, so they are redoing it correctly.

Another big concern I have is the dumbing down of American society. I am utterly appalled at the lack of knowledge folks have in regarding to American history, US geography, US government, economics, current events, etc. – the exact subjects one must have a good handle on if one is to vote objectively. I have spent a big part of my life living in Alaska. Occasionally, in a casual conversation with someone down in the lower 48 states, I get asked where I live – to which I would answer "Alaska." Most folks get all interested because "Alaska" seems to be a magical word. In general, most folks say something like "it sure is cold up there isn't it?" to which I explain that Alaska has a wonderful summer. But what scares me is when I get asked serious questions like "Now, tell me where is Alaska?" or "Is it part of the USA?" or "What language do they speak there?" And these are US citizens who vote! I might expect questions like that if I was to say that I was from Bhutan but not a state in the USA. Another example of not staying sufficiently informed came from the time I was on a Greyhound bus from El Paso, TX, to Deming, NM. Seated behind me was a 10-yr-old girl with her extended family traveling cross country from Atlanta to Los Angeles. We took Interstate Highway 10 which follows the Mexican/USA border and then enters New Mexico. The little gal was totally confused by the signs that said Mexico on the left side of the bus and then the new sign ahead that said "Entering New Mexico," so she asked her parents what was the difference. There was a long silence and then she shouted back to her grandparents in the row of seats behind her and asked the same question since her folks had no answer. Again, there was a long silence. When I couldn't take it any more I turned around and explained to the poor child what was going on. She then passed this info along to her family. And those two generations are American voters!

It was at that point in my life that I decided the USA really needs to make some changes to the voting privilege since people are not acting responsibly to stay educated or informed. Obviously, folks who know nothing of Alaska or New Mexico or Mexico are not informed. I would hate to embarrass them by asking simple questions like: "What does the secretary of state do?" or "How many senators are there?" or "In what decade did World War II end?" Our country's first generations had a keen interest in the development of their country and the issues at hand. They understood that a Republic only works when its population remains knowledgeable enough to be able to vote with the country's best interest in mind. *"No people will tamely surrender their liberties, nor can any be easily subdued, when knowledge is diffused and virtue is preserved. On the contrary, when people are universally ignorant, and debauched in their manners, they will sink under their own weight without the aid of foreign invaders."* – Samuel Adams 1775

While schools do an atrocious job of teaching American history and US government, what I find far worse is the news media with its left-wing bias and Democratic Party collusion. I have gotten sick of this arm of the establishment attempting to shove propaganda down our throats or create some alternate reality. We no longer have real news but a daily invented soap opera that fits their socialist narrative. Gone are the days of straight news reporting in a brief 30-minute radio or TV program. The "Only the facts mam, only the facts" formula has been replaced by all-day news programs that fill the time with "experts" giving us their opinions and interpretation of issues. I could really care less what some so-called "expert" thinks on an issue. "Second guessing" is not news reporting, so why even call it that. The media as morphed into nothing more than a stupid talk show. My favorite newspaper used to be the *The Wall Street Journal* because on the single front page you had all the important news items of the day in a concise clipped format. Real news stories mind you, not fake and made-up stories as is common practice in today's world. Invented stories just to grab your attention. Current day news writers and reporters add in so much drivel I believe they must be paid by the word. They use this drivel to push their left-wing agenda and the gullible public simply absorbs it as fact without ever investigating it for themselves. It is nothing more than plain and simple brainwashing. Maybe the news agencies should initiate a policy that names a set price for a news piece of say 300 words in length. For every word over that amount, some dollar amount is subtracted. Maybe this would force writers to be more concise and factual. If it can't be fact checked and verified by two actual real-life witnesses (minimum required in *Deuteronomy* 19:15 to convict), then the "news story" shouldn't even be printed. And, if it comes out later that any part of the article was false or misleading, the reporter should not only lose any and all income from that article, but both the reporter and his/her news agencies should be heavily fined. If this were to be implemented, the media folks would all be out of business within days. To lie in court carries a heavy penalty for perjury, maybe we should hold the media to the same kind of standard. That might cause them to think twice about what they print. The First Amendment of the Constitution, which prohibits the "abridging the freedom of speech, or of the press," doesn't justify lying about everything as the media do now. Individuals certainly have the right to have whatever opinion they so desire, even if it's void of any evidential support, but the news should be the simple unbiased truth not fairy tales or political propaganda.

Government handouts are another real problem in slanting the voting public toward the left and toward tyranny. Who would dare bite the hand of the person (or government) who feeds them. These transfer payment programs (everything from Social Security on down) do little except buy voters and create dependency. Without exception, the recipients will always vote for leftists (socialists) who will leave their program in place and hopefully even augment it. This sad state of affairs has brought us socialism and moral decay, and has condemned the country to a miserable financial decline. Many defend these programs with "it is my money – I paid for it" etc. Well fine, as I said in the section on Social Security, let's give it back to them with interest. Do you think people will accept this? I doubt it – they want the 1000% Ponzi scheme return. Everyone has turned greedy. They care little about what was best for the country or is fair to future generations.

A second aspect of the government handout problem that I see has to do with government workers. They are a huge voting block, some 22 million, nearly double the nation's manufacturing sector (2016 numbers: www.bls.gov). How do you think they are inclined to vote? To preserve and grow their cushy jobs or to bring us back to Constitution-based limited government? Government workers typically gain several times the wage of an equivalent job in the private sector and that is without even adding in these ridiculous retirement plans and all the lobbyists' goodies thrown in. I equate the overpay in government jobs with welfare support. Many times there is no common sense reason for the government job in the first place or we can most certainly do fine without it or half the amount of employees. While government employees do work, they typically do it in s-l-o-w motion. They have no incentive because the government has a self-proclaimed monopoly on the services they provide, so why be expedient. For example, how many times have you been frustrated to no end waiting in line at the Department of Motor Vehicles to register your car or renew your driver's license only to see the employees behind the counter dilly dallying around, chatting, and playing with their stupid tablet phones. If they were to get paid the same as an equivalent job in the private sector, I feel that even this would be too much, since, in reality, they only put out half the work.

How preposterously our public **"servants"** are overpaid reminds me of a food stamp program California had some 50 years ago. In that program, a low-income person could buy food stamps valued at $200 with $40 (or something like that). Same thing with government employees – with $40 of work they are getting $200 in pay. I remember a news article a few years back about a Ventura County, CA, sheriff who had recently retired and was suing the county (his boss) because of a $90,000 bonus shortfall in his retirement pay, all the while he was receiving $250,000 a year in retirement benefits. I can't even imagine gaining $250,000 over three-quarters of a decade of working my butt off, much less to receive that much per year in "retirement." Something stinks bad and needs to be cleaned up. Maybe we need to match government job wages to the mid-range price for a comparable private sector job. So, for a sheriff, maybe we should make a survey of how much the head honcho at a private security company makes and pay them more or less along those lines. And drop all these government pensions – go get your own. The sheriff's offices would sure get a lot fewer job applicants since everyone knows the primary reason folks want a government job is for a ride on the gravy train. In the country where I was living as a volunteer, the police and military make only a taste more than a private security guard. Another good option would be to privatize police, fire, air traffic, building inspectors, etc. Cut out the fat. Ever notice how many public "servants" end up retiring as millionaires from a government job? I can name more than a few in Congress. Should there really be such disparity between the electorate and the elected? To serve as a police officer in an area like the south side of Chicago many may consider a high-risk job, but in reality it is way way down the list as far as the most dangerous jobs are concerned. Fishermen and loggers are 10 times more likely to be killed on the job than a police officer, a pilot is 5 times as likely, a roofer is 4 times as likely, an iron worker or a garbage man is 3 times as likely, a truck driver or farmer is 2 times as likely, etc. (Police work isn't as dangerous as you may think – *The Huffington Post* January 15, 2015). They don't include rough framers specifically in the Bureau of Labor Statistics but you can bet we are way up there, at least on a par with a roofer (www.bls,gov). All these "more dangerous" private sector jobs make only a small fraction of what a public servant like a police officer or firefighter receives. The risk of physical harm faced daily on most construction jobs is extremely high, and, over my life, I have heard of many jobsite deaths. I know of no other career including military service where the risk of ending up disabled is as high as in construction. One in eight of us construction workers will end up disabled.

I believe that college-age students are one of the greatest problems our voting system faces today, mainly because these youngsters are totally void of any real-life experience and lack common sense. After every presidential election where these poor little kids' socialist choice doesn't win, they are out in the streets rioting. They appear to be nothing more than a bunch of spoiled brats who have no idea how our republic works and why. I thank God for the wisdom of the founders who understood how self-destructive pure democratic power was, so they created four power centers in the US government (President, HR, Senate, Supreme Court), and, in its original intent, only the HR was directly elected by the people. These juveniles have no idea how blessed they are that most states' legislatures let the people directly participate in choosing the Presidential Electors when it certainly isn't mandatory. The Electoral College system does a good job of restricting a few high-population centers from dictating terms to the whole country, which is exactly what these immature kids want. Most city slickers have little to no knowledge about the real "engine room" of the country where food, materials, and energy are produced, yet by mob rule (democratic popular vote), these folks could actually vote to kill themselves if it wasn't for the system put in place in 1787.

Hardly a student nowadays has passed through the maturing stage of struggling to pay living expenses or worrying about making ends meet. It gives one a whole different perspective on life. This is not true of past generations who grew up working on the farm, etc. I was lucky like them and had my first "paying" job when I was 13 years old. It was a Friday after school through Sunday afternoon deal. My brother and I washed dishes, mopped the floor, and set and cleaned the dining room at a Catholic Retreat home. We loved it, especially because we were allowed to eat anything left untouched on the attendee's plates when we cleared the tables after each meal. They served much better food to the attendees than we ate at home, so we scarfed down any and every morsel. We already did jobs on the farm, so work in that sense was no big deal, but this was the first job we actually got cash money. Of course, the small amount we earned went to our mom to help with the family bills, but it taught us much about life and gave us a sense of the real world we would be thrown into shortly. Just 4 years later, at 17 years old, I was self-sufficient, living on my own, and building houses. It was tough, but you grow up real fast in that kind of circumstance. Kids nowadays don't have that same opportunity, and far too many keep a hold of mommy's skirt until they are nearing 30 years old. Only then do they venture out slowly and begin to get a real taste of life. Colleges also fill their minds with left-wing mush, producing students who are brainwashed and totally inept to analyze anything on their own. It used to be that schools taught folks to think for themselves (critical thinking). Students were expected to find out and solve things. Now, it is more about learning the left-wing position on everything from the environment to globalization (*The Closing of the American Mind* – Allan Bloom). Today's college students are less than dumb. A Zogby International study done in 2002 for the Princeton's National Association of Scholars confirmed that high school graduates of the

1950s did approximately the same on a general information test as college seniors of today. The National Geographic and Roper Public Affairs 2006 geographic literacy survey (a survey of college age 18 to 24 year old) showed that less than 50% could identify New York and Ohio on a US map. Only 40% could find Iraq or Saudi Arabia on a Middle East map, and only 25% could find Iran or Israel. A study done by the American Institutes for Research revealed that a bare 20% of four-year college students had any command over basic mathematics. Certainly don't ask them about our Constitution or American history unless you want to throw up. Yet, these folks are allowed to vote? Vote for what? *"Too much of what is called 'education' is little more than an expensive isolation from reality."* – Thomas Sowell

So here are my wild ideas to clean up voting. While it is unlikely any of them will ever see the light of day, it is nonetheless how I see things. Voting is the most important thing we as regular citizens can do and it must be taken seriously. Our choices should be educated and selfless, focused only on what is best for the country's future. Unfortunately, both of these qualities are lacking in the US voting system today. Back in the day when universal suffrage was enacted, there were no welfare systems in place and everyone survived by their own sweat. People had a keen interest in allowing the economy to operate so they could better themselves, and desired to keep government spending, regulation, and power to a bare minimum. Granted, there were poor laws that helped the less fortunate, but able-bodied unemployed poor were given work in workhouses, while folks disabled by age or injury were given help in various ways, but mostly this was done in a sectarian setting. Since socialist welfare programs began to be enacted in 1935, we have seen the voting system become polluted. It now serves mainly as a method to perpetuate and multiply the power of the elite left. So, first on my cleanup list would be to deny voting privileges altogether to everyone who receives any form of government welfare since their vote has been bought. They use voting as a method to give themselves gifts that are paid for by someone else. They have no "stick in the fire" as the saying goes. Second, I would like to see the votes of government workers (other than military) count for less than an individual working in the private sector, since their voting inclination has generally more to do with their own personal job preservation or betterment than for the good of the country as a whole. Maybe something along the lines of the percentage an employee in the public sector earns compared to what an equivalent job in the government sector earns. Half or two-thirds of a full vote. Third, I would limit voting in the private sector (the engine room of the nation) to those folks who are paying income taxes. This would wash out both the young student who is clueless and the older folks on Social Security whose principle purpose in voting is to keep their Social Security and Medicare payments from being disrupted. Fourth, after this leaning out process, those remaining must pass a simple test to verify that they have enough basic knowledge of the US government, American history, economics, current events, etc., to be objective. Voting is a privilege, not some God-given right and, like any privilege, it carries responsibility. If you will not carry the responsibility, then you should not have the privilege. The privilege of driving a car requires that one attain a certain level of mastery over the subject matter, and then pass both a written and practical test. How can it be that the privilege of voting, which carries an even heavier responsibility, has no requirement at all except to be breathing. Most people are plain clueless about what is going on. They are too lazy and disinterested to even pick up a book on economics, American history, etc. This simple requirement would force folks to at least pay a little attention to what is going on. In this way, we might start getting folks who vote for the good of the country, not more food stamps. Fifth, only the legal citizens of a state should be used in assigning the number of Electoral College votes, not the results from a general population census that includes illegal aliens. This is screwing up big time the value of citizens' votes. Sixth, everyone who desires to vote must present a state-issued ID that clearly shows whether the holder is a citizen or not. Even Third World countries operate in this fashion. The 2013 McLaughlin & Associates scientific bilingual poll of Hispanic adults in the USA showed that 13% of the noncitizens were registered to vote. Obviously, this is why the Democratic Party doesn't want to clean up voting.

I am most certainly concerned to have Muslims voting since their primary interest is to replace the US Constitution with Islam's sharia law, but as I proposed in the immigration section – if they can't denounce sharia law from the "get go" then they should be sent packing, and this alone would eliminate the detrimental effect of their vote against our country principles.

"Not everything that is faced can be changed, but nothing can be changed until it is faced."   – James Baldwin

National Defense

THERE IS MUCH DISCUSSION on the level and purpose of national defense. Personally, I was sorely disappointed when George W. Bush and a lame duck Congress decided to create the Department of Homeland Security (DHS) in 2002. With one swipe of his pen, President Bush forever enlarged the size and scope of the federal government. Supposedly this was needed to keep us "safe" and protect us from terrorism, but I have my doubts. What in the hell is the Department of Defense (DoD) supposed to do? Check out their mission statement "... *protect the security of our country.*" Why couldn't they be mobilized or conscripted to deal with the threat. To me, it is nothing more than a 65 billion dollar a year waste (2016 budget, www.crs.gov). If you profile and don't let Muslims in your house (USA) from the beginning, we wouldn't have to hire a whole bunch of new guys (DHS) to follow them around and make sure they don't cause any trouble. Now we have created a police state. Muslims have been trouble makers all though world history, did folks just think they would stop all the bad stuff they do and act civilized once they were allowed to immigrate to the USA? The Islamic nations of Morocco, Algiers, Tunis, and Tripoli were the very first enemies of the newly formed USA and we fought them during the 15 year Barbary Wars. Our nation's first exposure to Islam was unwaveringly negative, and the forefathers shared my same belief that Islam is totally incompatibility with our nation. "*The ambassador answered us that [the right] was founded on the Laws of the Prophet, that it was written in their Koran, that all nations who should not have answered their authority were sinners, that it was their right and duty to make war upon them wherever they could be found, and to make slaves of all they could take as prisoners, and that every Mussulman who should be slain in battle was sure to go to Paradise,"* – Thomas Jefferson wrote this to the Secretary of State John Jay, explaining that peace with them was impossible. Personally, I feel that Muslims in the USA today, aside from the need to denounce sharia law or leave, should pay a special yearly "Muslim tax" to help cover the cost of operating the DHS which was created solely to babysit them. Call it a use tax if you like. Before we started letting Muslims through the door in mass, we had no need for a DHS. Why should we non-Muslims have to pay for their babysitting service? Muslims refuse to stand up to the radicalization in their own religion. Why? They can't disagree because this murderous behavior is laid out in their own Quran and if they "really" do object (as opposed to just doing it as "Taqiyya") they risk getting their head cut off by their own people. The radicals follow the Quran down to the word. You certainly don't see Muslim imams condemning terrorism. Nor do you see US citizens who are Muslims forming citizen patrols so they can fight and stamp out these radicalized elements. Of course not. US Muslim organizations routinely reject funds offered by the DHS under the Countering Violent Extremism (CVE) program to help them produce literature and films countering Islamic extremism. It's pretty obvious why they won't accept the funds – they don't want it to stop. False propaganda groups like the CAIR (Council on American-Islamic Relations) whose sole purpose is to go around spreading a rosy false narrative of Islam together with the terrorist front group Muslim Brotherhood should be tossed out of the USA on their heads.

You may not realize it, but the terrorists have already achieved a strategic victory over our culture – we are now terrorized by our own government everyday as a result of Islam. Think of that every time you pass through a TSA (Transport Security Administration) airport security checkpoint and strip down. It used to be nice to travel by air, now it is a nightmare. And the simple reason – Muslim terrorists. Our government simply refuses to profile and instead must "hassle" everyone equally. What a joke! We should look at little tighter at folks from the Mideast and leave us real Americans alone. Like many of you, my family shed its blood to build this country – why in God's name would we want to tear it down. We have no allegiance to Islam. After 9/11 the federal government consulted Israel on how to protect the USA from Muslim terrorists. Israel shared the obvious – you must profile – but the USA couldn't adopt that policy because of all this "political correctness" BS. And, who do you think is to blame for the added security fees on your airline ticket?

I hear folks talk all the time about how we need to spend more money on defense because we are falling behind other nations militarily. They claim that we don't have enough soldiers, that we don't have as many boats and aircraft as in the old days, and that what we do have is falling apart and outdated. I would like to address each of these objections separately.

First, I would like to ask "how can we be falling behind militarily if we spend more on national defense than the next seven countries combined?" Yes, the USA spent some $596 billion in 2015 on national defense, while China, Saudi Arabia, Russia, United Kingdom, India, France, and Japan **combined** spend only $567 billion (Peter G Peterson Foundation – 2016 Fiscal Summit). That being said, we should be absolutely untouchable militarily. If we aren't, then there must be a lot of mismanagement. Some have opined that the DoD has lost track of near 10 "trillion" dollars over the past 20 years by poor accounting practices alone. The DoD should be audited so we can find and correct the blatant misuse of funds. The USA needs a lean, mean, fighting machine not some fat, bloated monster. If we did away with buying the figurative $150 hammer and nixed some of these questionable high-cost development programs (come on now – $800,000 a pop for each ammo shell for the new Zumwalt class destroyer or the insanely high-priced 1.5 trillion F-35 fighter program), we might just begin to get things under control. Of course, this means we will also need to wean the defense contractors from the tit which will ruffle all kinds of feathers. The military must learn to focus in terms of the "best return for the buck" just like the regular Joe must do in the real world. They must learn to be practical and frugal. If something can be done cheaper in the private sector then maybe it should be done there. I have no qualms about developing new ideas, but they should be reasonable ideas within a sane financial budget. Possibly we can find a way to shift more of these development ideas to the private sector's dollar rather than using the taxpayer's hard-earned cash. The USA is so deep in debt right now that we should be focused on cutting budgets not growing them.

Another issue with which I have an issue is training costs. Do the military pilots pay back the USAF for any part of the very costly training that puts them directly into a near $200,000 private sector airline job as soon as they leave the service? The same holds true for doctors and the like whom the taxpayers send thru high-cost medical or specialty schools only to have them jump ship directly into a high-paying private practice after just a short tour of duty. Schooling of this type that is funded directly out of the military's budget should be seriously scrutinized, since the recipients are actually receiving hundreds of thousands of dollars in extra benefits that are not included in their pay. I personally know guys from the two situations just mentioned. Their military service has helped them make a lot of money on the outside. I will never downplay anyone's service to this country, but I do believe that what we taxpayers do/did to advance their private sector careers should be taken into consideration. How fair is it to the US taxpayer who does pay his own way through these same schools and as a result will suffer immense debt for decades?

Second, I find it truly amazing that politicians and presidential candidates talk about the need to up the number of Navy ships and aircraft. They note that we now have less of these assets than we did in 1948 or some date back in time. They fail to take into account that one modern day aircraft carrier can literally annihilate with ease a whole fleet of ships from several decades back. Same with aircraft. A single F-18 with advanced weaponry could knock out a whole squadron of those antique planes without even working up a sweat. You can't compare apples with oranges. Number of assets does not signify power or strength. Wouldn't you rather have a single hydrogen bomb than 10,000 general purpose TNT-type bombs. Today, with fewer boats and planes, we are infinitely more deadly than we were just a few decades back. We have fighters like the stealth F22, bombers like the invisible B2, and warships like the Arleigh Burke class destroyer or Ford class aircraft carrier that are the envy of every other nation on the planet.

These same politicians also love to make misleading statements about our bombers. They say that our bombers are all twice as old as the pilots flying them and we need new ones. They speak in half-truths. While the B52 bomber design is from the 1950s she has been constantly upgraded with the latest in avionics, air defense systems, delivery apparatus, etc. In truth, she is an amazing aircraft but is only one of the three bomber types on the USAF current heavy bomber asset list (B1, B2, B52). Think of the B52 like the vulnerable DHC2 Beaver. Maybe some of you have seen a DeHavilland Beaver. I have been blessed to fly her some in Alaska. The Beaver was designed in the late 1940s and manufactured until 1967. She uses an old radial engine that dates back to 1929. She is one of those once-in-a-lifetime designs that is worth their weight in gold. Today some 50 years after the last one came out the factory's door, there is still no other aircraft in her class that can equal her performance, payload, and economy.

Flying the De Havilland Beaver off the Nuyakuk River in Alaska (2008)

The B52 is just like that. She remains an effective and economical heavy bomber in the absence of sophisticated air defense and is expected to have a service life out to 2040. Why would you ever want to replace her if she is still fulfilling her mission? The B52 is sent in to bomb an area when all the air defenses have been knocked out and the USAF enjoys total air superiority. If that is not the case, then we fire up the trick B1 or B2 heavy bombers that are built to penetrate an enemy's air defenses. The B52 is like the versatile jobsite pickup truck. She is designed to carry a load and drop it on target when no one is in the way, while the B1 and B2 are sneaky little bastards that will slip right by you and drop their load even when you are standing in front of them on high alert. The USAF hates to use these two fancy bombers unless they are really needed since, if by chance, they get shot down, the USAF just erased $1.7 billion if a B2 or $400 million if a B1 (2016 dollars for both www.af.mil) off their balance sheets. They wisely prefer to dispatch a bunch of less expensive fighters to knock out all the enemy's air defenses and then send in the less expensive B52 that are "only" worth a mere $88 million each. Then again, the wars we have been involved in lately rarely call for the big guys. Most of the time the fighters can be used to pinpoint bomb factories, a caravan of trucks, etc.

Third, in response to the line that we need to spend more cash on the military because "we are becoming short-handed personnel-wise and many of our aircraft are falling apart," I have this to say – "What do you expect happens if you are constantly getting into wars all over the map?" If our highly trained service personnel get killed in some stupid war, then we must begin from scratch again to train up a newbie. This costs big bucks and takes many years. And unfortunately equipment does wear out and requires maintenance or replacement when you use it. If you only drove your work truck 10,000 miles a year it would last a lot longer than if you are driving it 10,000 miles a month. Doesn't take a genius to figure that out. What we need to do is stop getting into absurd wars that have nothing to do with protecting our country or her interests. This would give our military the chance to regroup, and the equipment would last as it should. A strong military is a deterrent, not something you must use because you have it. Maybe you have a gun in your home for personal protection. I hope so. It will probably sit there through your whole life and never be used, but it is available just in case. And just because you have one, doesn't mean you have to go out and try to gun down all the bad guys running around. They will get theirs when they come to your house to do harm. In President George Washington's Farewell Address (1796) he warned against getting entangled in foreign wars, but the leaders of today have failed to heed his wisdom. They may have fallen prey to the defense contractors' big lobby. War is good for them, and they like it when you use something up and must fix or replace it. But what about using up our young men and women's lives? The Obama administration, "supposedly" dedicated to peace (with Obama himself winning the 2009 Nobel Peace), was involved in war every single day they were in power – an absolute travesty. Many recent presidents have forgotten that only Congress has the power to declare war. These presidents side-step this limitation and involve us in all kinds of "undeclared wars" by purposely misinterpreting the War Powers Act which was drafted solely to allow the president to be able quickly defend the US homeland from sudden attack.

> "Wherever the standard of freedom and independence has been or shall be unfurled there will America's hearts, her benedictions, and her prayers be. But she goes not abroad in search of monsters to destroy. She is the well-wisher of the freedom and independence of all. She is the champion and vindicator only of her own."   – John Quincy Adams

While some Muslims may have served honorably in the armed forces, I believe that no Muslim should ever be allowed to serve in the US Military. Not only are they unable to assimilate into military society without all their beards, turbans, hijabs, etc. (which clearly shows where their allegiance lies), but history has shown how horrific an error this is via the innumerous attacks or conspiring to attack the military by former or active duty US Muslim soldiers (i.e., Nidal Hasan, Hasan Akbar, Abu Khalid Abdul-Latif, Tairod Nathan Webster Pugh, Hasan Edmonds, Ali Mohamed, Semi Osman, Jeffrey Leon Battle, Hassan Abu-Jihaad, and Naser Jason Abdo). Even if they don't kill US soldiers or help kill US soldiers while they are in the military service, they are most certainly being equipped with deadly skills that will allow them to wage jihad against us down the road. What kind of sense does this make? Why should we take that kind of risk? How did this work out when we trained guys like Saddam Hussein, Manuel Noriega, or Osama Bin Laden, only to have them turn around and bite us in the butt. I mourn the many young men and women who lost their lives to correct these asinine decisions. We must wake up. It would be a lot simpler if we just don't train questionable or risky folks from the start. And whose stupid idea was it to change our country's centuries-old military standards to accommodate a few Muslims anyway? The military isn't some kind of social experiment to be governed by political correctness. If you don't like the rules, don't play the game (don't enlist).

Environmentalists and the Global Warming Hoax

"It's easier to fool people than to convince them that they have
been fooled." — Mark Twain

"FROM 1880 TO 2015, *the [earth's] temperature has
increased from 288 K [degrees Kelvin] to 288.8 K, a 0.3% increase.
I think the temperature has been amazingly stable. ... What is the
optimal temperature for the Earth? Is it the temperature we have
right now? That would be a miracle. Maybe it's two degrees warmer.
Maybe it's two degrees colder. No one has told me what the optimal
temperature is for the whole Earth.*" Ivar Giaever (Nobel laureate
in Physics)

I view the current "global warming" malarkey (or their new
buzzword "climate change") as nothing more than confused people
running on emotion rather than thinking rationally. They can't see
the sky for the clouds. You can believe anything you want, but that
doesn't make it true. Throughout all history the earth's temperature has fluctuated up and down. I don't know the range and neither
does anyone else, because nobody was here throughout the earth's
long history to record it. If that is so, what kind of phony data did
the scientists use to set up their brainless computer models? It is
impossible for them to consider all the variables because they don't
even know them all. To "make believe" that man can do anything

to greatly affect this planet's climate is nothing short of maniacal. It would be like blaming a bunch of ants that lived near your house for the wind blowing off your roof. Governments have now spent into the trillions to combat "global warming," yet even with all this money it hasn't made a speck of difference. It has only caused them to cry for more money to battle this hoax while they disregard the real facts that show the earth's temperature has not moved an iota for nearly two decades. Instead of chasing made-up fantasies, this money could have been spent to help some of the real problems the world faces like malaria, Ebola virus disease, or AIDS. Stay with me as I share a few thoughts. Please note that the earth has never made/ makes the exact same circular track around the sun, neither does it spin perfectly on its axis – these variables have and will continually change throughout all time. Run a mile around a high school track. In each of those four laps you were never in the exact same place more than once – you varied every lap. So now if you consider that even the slightest variation in distance from the sun or tilt of the axis affects the angle of and amount of the sun's rays that hit and warm the earth, you can easily conclude that there will always be variations in temperature. Now, throw in things like sunspot flare-ups in unknown times in the past or ones that will happen in the future, and you can begin to see the complexity in making any type of accurate assessment going forward. Even other stars have affected and will affect the sun's gravitational pull on the earth and its orbit.

We know that sometime in the past the earth went through radical climatic changes since we have a tiny glimpse of it through fossil records. Nearly all the earth's surface was green when dinosaurs roamed the earth, and then suddenly they all died off when the earth became glaciated during the Ice Age. Good thing it swung back from that period, because I don't like cold weather much. According to captain's records from the early 1800s, ships easily plied the Arctic waters as they searched for a Northwest passage, and then only a few years later the same area was found choked by ice. So, no one has even the slightest clue to how temperatures have come and gone, or what the earth's perfect temperature is, yet various "scientists" (who depend on government grants to make their living – something that should stop) acting as God are claiming that the world is heating up and that man's pollution is the cause. This theory fits the left's scare tactic agenda, so it is pushed and the "save the world" movement continues in spite of evidence that it is a farce and the numbers were manipulated (*Daily Mail* February 6, 2017). They depend on people being ignorant and gullible. How can any scientist possibly quantize the real amount of pollutants that a single volcano eruption spews forth, much less the 50 to 60 eruptions that occur each month (Smithsonian Institution – Global Volcanism Network)? Most certainly this affects the heating and cooling of the earth. The oceans are not rising as they predicted, the southern polar cap is not shrinking as they predicted but rather growing, so there are some definite inconsistencies. Data recently showed that, in reality, we have been in a cooling trend for the past 18 years. Russian scientific studies predict the beginning of a new ice age by 2030 due to a recent drop in the sun's magnetic activity (Valentina Zharkova from North Umbria University). So the scientists are absolutely clueless to predict the future climate with their fancy computer models and it will always be that way. Knowing the future will always be God's realm. *"For the wisdom of this world is foolishness in God's sight. As it is written: He catches the wise in their craftiness."* (1 *Corinthians* 3:19)

What truly amazes me is the resiliency of the earth. Nowhere can it be seen more clearly than where I lived for a while in the tropics. You cut all the plants back around your house, but after just one rainy season the jungle is back fighting to devour your house like a lava monster. Can't say that for the desert, but the jungle always reclaims itself. You must understand that I am not saying that man does not have an effect on the planet, but, in the big scheme of things, it is inconsequential and hardly worth mentioning.

One thing that really irks me is that the Feds have been messing around with the atmosphere for over 30 years behind our backs using varying types of stratospheric aerosol spraying to reflect sunlight, seed clouds, etc., in an attempt to "save the planet" in their crazy words. Not only is what they are doing untestable, but it is as dangerous as hell. As a result of their utter stupidity, they have magnified normal weather changes and have brought on droughts, caused a loss of blue sky, exposed both plants and animals to hazardous chemicals, and created conditions that are more conducive to explosive wildfires because of the widespread dispersion of ingredients like magnesium.

Some folks make a big deal when they find of a taste higher CO_2 count in the atmosphere than what they believe has been the historical norm. Seems they have forgotten high school science class, since this is exactly what plant life needs to live. The plants are digging it. It is like receiving a little more ice cream on your plate than you were expecting. And then all this ruckus about how we humans are cutting down all the trees, etc. An overexaggeration to say the least. It certainly fails to take into account that one tree produces thousands of seedlings and is constantly mega-propagating itself. Yeah, some trees do get cut down to build things (good for us carpenters) but forest management is pretty high tech nowadays, as is firefighting, so many forests are much larger today than they were 200 years ago. Southern Chile, for example, is now covered with pine tree plantations where before it was just bare shrub land. In fact, many natural forests today are in desperate need of thinning. They are so thick that they are choking themselves off because sunlight can't get in. The animals that lived there have all headed off to other places where they don't need a machete just to move around. In earlier times, this thinning process was done by uncontrolled lightning fires and massive areas the size of whole states would go up in flames. This was good, because it allowed the natural cycle of forest life to do its thing and animals would return. But I suppose according to the environmentalist it is bad if man does the same thing by logging and uses the wood for homes. If you are ever in Oakland, CA, visit the downtown library where hopefully they still have an old black-and-white photo of the whole Bay Area taken in the 1800s from the Oakland Hills hanging on the wall. I love that photo because one can trek up the hill to the exact same spot where it was originally taken and compare it against the phenomenal changes that have taken place in the Bay since that time. Kind of like a 200-year time-lapse photograph. The thing that struck me most in this old photo was that all the vacant hills and mountains (Mt. Tamalpais, etc.) are just grassy knolls – there is hardly a tree to be seen. Yet as I look out over this same scene today, there are trees all over the place in spite of the immense urban expansion. Something to ponder.

"Where we have strong emotions, we're liable to fool ourselves."   – Carl Sagan

I have found environmentalists to be far from open-minded people. Most are just taught some party line to spout to the general public by their leaders. Most are clueless about the earth's natural processes and incapable of deductive reasoning. Take weather, for example. Weather is one subject that we pilots are expected to master. We all learn that weather is caused by the uneven heating and cooling of the earth's surface. This unevenness causes rising and falling air. The sun's rays striking an asphalt parking lot will cause more rising air as compared to a lake or forest. So when an environmentalist sharing information outside Trader Joes in Seattle tells me that Seattle is hotter today than it used to be, I reply with "I can see that, but tell me what has changed about Seattle itself since those earlier days?" I have never had an environmentalist grab my lead because they are so focused on their talking points. Granted, there may be a few more pollutants in the air today than yesterday, and while this may have a near invisible micro-mini effect on weather, the obvious much grander cause-and-effect influences are overlooked. Consider that Seattle has grown rapidly in size as a city and now there are many more parking lots, buildings, malls, freeways, parked cars, etc. heating the air as compared to a few years back when it was smaller. As a result there has been a major change to the amount of lifted air which, in turn, will modify the local weather patterns slightly. You have most certainly heard the term "micro climate" – it is when natural features on the earth's surface produce a localized weather phenomenon. The Seattle weather change is just one small example of how man-made features can also effect similar changes.

I have found environmentalists to be downright self-centered. Few of them care what a local population may want for themselves in respect to the development of a local asset and go about blocking it in spite of 100% local approval. Take, for example, the Pebble Mine in Alaska. It is one of the richest mineral finds in recent history whose development is heavily supported by the local population, but totally opposed by people from the lower 48 states. These environmentalists play the media game to whip up national opposition by spinning all kinds of fantasy stories of the ecological damage that it will supposedly cause. It is nothing more than an offshoot of the much larger international global warming fraud. The locals want the jobs and business that the new mine will create so they can survive in this harsh part of the world. How unfair it is to have other people dictate your life by fabricated lies. I have been blessed to fly most summers in the Alaskan bush since 1989. I have worked for mines, hunting outfits, logging camps, fishing processors, etc., all over the state. For several seasons,

I worked onsite at a Placer Dome Inc. mine located along Donlin Creek (Alaska interior), so I can speak first hand to the amount of care and concern that is spent in preserving and bettering the natural environment. Where Placer Dome Inc. mines, the rivers are cleaner after they leave than before they arrived. I have also worked for various other mines along the north side of the Alaska Range west of Delta Junction and they were just as conscientious and meticulous.

Delivering fuel to a mine at Virginia creek near Delta Junction, Alaska (1998)

The deceitful environmentalists have pretty much killed the drift-net swordfish fishing business off the coast of central and southern California. They would run advertisements showing a baby seal all wrapped up in a fishing net, commenting that these poor innocent creatures along with Flipper the Dolphin are getting killed as collateral damage to gill-net fishing and thus this method of fishing must be outlawed. And all the people watching their TVs are in tears and vote to shut it down, little knowing that these ads were nothing but a big lie. I worked a couple seasons as a drift-net swordfish spotting pilot. Well, I didn't really spot swordfish, I simply found the areas where the fish might be hanging out so the boats could try their luck there at night. I would also spy from the sky on other fishing groups when they were pulling their nets to see if they were "in the fish" so I know damn well what gets trapped in swordfish fishing nets.

Swordfish spotting off the coast of California (1991)

The ignorant public has no idea that the hole size of a net's mesh varies with what type of fish one desires to catch. So, if a fisherman is trying to catch swordfish, the net's grid-like structure is made with huge holes since swordfish are big fish. Drift-net fishing of swordfish is done in open water some 20 to 40 miles offshore. It is done at night when swordfish can't see the net. The net is then pulled at first light when it becomes visible to the swordfish and they easily avoid it. Hopefully, a few swordfish get hung up on the net during the night. It is a hard thankless job. Two things to consider. A seal would not normally be that far out at sea unless he got disoriented (doesn't happen), and a seal does not drift around at night on the high seas so as to get snagged in a net. The point is that the seal and the swordfish are not found in the same area! You will never hear that truth from the environmentalists for they have an agenda and damned be the truth. While Flipper might be in the area swimming around, he will never get trapped in a drift-net because he operates like a submarine with sonar. If his sonar return shows something in the way he goes around or under it. In all my time spying on other fishing groups plus recording what my own group caught, I have never seen anything caught but swordfish, a few sharks, and maybe once or twice a large sea turtle. The shark and sea turtle get caught in the net because they are more or less the same size as the swordfish. These poor fishermen don't have the funds or media connections to defend themselves against these masters of deception.

To finalize this section, I who am not an environmentalist, am in the end a better environmentalist than the wackos. I have always lived very simply, purchased only what I absolutely need to survive, rented just a small studio or a one-bedroom apartment, and have used foot or pedal power as much as possible. I kept the same work truck for 35 years, so I have not added to our nation's refuse pile nor have I required new materials to be mined and processed in order to build me a new SUV of the type that all the environmentalists must have. Their vehicles easily identified having oil-based plastic kayaks fastened to their roof racks and oil-based neoprene wetsuits tossed in the back. Of course, the most devout have electric cars, which they believe do not pollute the environment, little knowing that the CO_2 (that stuff that they believe is so bad) generated just in the production of their car's special batteries would take a small V8 gas engine some 8 years to create (IVL Swedish Environmental Research Institute report), and this doesn't include the CO_2 produced by the coal- or natural gas–fed power plants that are called upon daily to recharge their batteries. What a joke! Practically everything I own, from my clothes on down to our household appliances, is recycled used gear from the thrift stores. I do not have a dog that the standard environmentalist keeps at his side at all times for the specific purpose to create small, smelly, natural packages for someone to step on. In the woods, we wonder why the water is now infested with *Giardia* when it is common knowledge that this was brought on by domesticated dog poop, likely from the same environmentalist's dog that left a package earlier today in the park. I could go on, but you get the idea. Their hypocrisy is totally preposterous.

I agree that we should take care of the earth and am a firm believer in "leave no trace" living. What I find amusing is how these same left-wing environmentalists who think man is the culprit and wish all humans (except them) be exterminated from the planet, are the same ones who are in favor of open-door unlimited immigration from Third World countries. They have no clue that the folks from these countries are the biggest polluters on the planet. Come visit a Third World country and you will see trash all over the place, on the sides of the roads, just everywhere. It looks like a ghetto. Why? Just plain lazy and selfish is how I see it. They buy something at the store to eat, unwrap it, and then discard the wrapper right where they stand, even if a trash receptacle is nearby. There is a volcano near where I lived in Central America that many people enjoyed climbing. It is real easy to climb, yet now and then someone gets lost climbing it. Not sure how they could possibly get lost for as I always told friends who wanted to climb the volcano – "just follow the trail of trash and it will lead you to the top". Kind of disheartening, but absolutely true. The locals who climb the volcano finish a store-bought bottle of H_2O and toss the empty container to the side of the trail. They eat a candy bar and there lies the wrapper, they defecate and there sits the used toilet paper. Environmental "storm troopers" is how I think of them.

"Would you bet your paycheck on a weather forecast for tomorrow? If not, then why should this country bet billions on global warming predictions that have even less foundation?"   – Thomas Sowell

The National Debt, a Balanced Budget, and the Money Supply

THOMAS JEFFERSON WROTE TO James Madison in 1789 – *"Then I say, the earth belongs to each of these generations during its course, fully and in its own right. The second generation receives it clear of the debts and encumbrances of the first, the third of the second, and so on. For if the first could charge it with a debt, then the earth would belong to the dead and not to the living generation. Then, no generation can contract debts greater than may be paid during the course of its own existence."*

How far we have traveled from this principle. Now an infinite number of unborn generations are on the hook to pay for something they had no part in incurring. They get the shaft from another huge Ponzi scheme.

The US national debt is approaching **$20 TRILLION** (actual "this minute" debt)! I can't even imagine a number that large. The height of a stack of 20,000,000,000,000 (twenty trillion) one dollar bills measures 1,357,320 miles. This would reach from the earth to the moon and back almost 3 times. And this doesn't take into account the additional $124 trillion of unfunded liability (owed at a future date for things like Social Security payments, etc.) which alone is a debt of over $1 million for each potential American worker today (www.statista.com, 2016 workforce 123.8 million, full time) or some $1.7 million that each millennial will need to come up with within 50 years. Absolutely shocking numbers that show the total ineptitude of the government in its handling of the American citizen's money and our nation's addiction to entitlements. The debt has grown to its current size as a result of all the "give me" transfer programs (socialism). During the past 50 years since welfare entitlements were enacted, we have spent $22 trillion on this insanity – **an amount roughly equal to the current national debt**. In 2017, government spending will exceed $4 trillion with 67% of this amount going for social causes including Social Security at $1 trillion, Medicare at $582 billion, Medicaid at $404 billion, and other miscellaneous forms of welfare combined (food stamps, unemployment compensation, child nutrition, child tax credits, supplemental security income, and student loans) at $550 billion (http://federal-budget.insidegov.com). This type of government spending far exceeds the authority of Congress as enumerated in Article I, Section 8, of the US Constitution. We have an increasingly bloated central government that is totally incapable of placing spending restrictions on itself, much less dealing with its own citizens' entitlement addiction problem. Government officials prefer to just keep upping the credit card limit (national debt) when it can't be paid. Totally insane! If a legislator wants to get elected or keep his cushy job when up for reelection, he better send some money to his district (buying votes) even if it must be borrowed. I see a huge lack of character in this country and its leaders. The little kid's practice of closing their eyes and covering their face when confronted with danger while exclaiming "what I can see won't hurt me" is practiced at all levels in our society. A government out of control and a selfish people. The nation's first president, George Washington, was adamant that, in order for the nation to stay strong, it must have a balanced budget and that any debt from war (the only legitimate reason to borrow) must be paid off immediately. Up until when Woodrow Wilson, the godfather of leftism, became president in

1913, the total government spending (federal, state, local) averaged less than 7% of the GDP. When FDR rammed socialism down everybody's throat during his time in office, total government spending soared to over 20% of the GDP (www.usgovernmentspending.com). Since then it has skyrocketed to over 40% of GDP with the vast amplification of the welfare state. The government is sucking up nearly half of the USA's total production, or, in other words, we are halfway to total socialism.

A government that was designed to do only a few specific things has now taken over everything. The principal responsibilities of the federal government as set forth in the Constitution were national defense and settling disputes between the states (interstate commerce, etc.). Sure, there were other little tasks assigned to it like creating a national currency, but my point is that it was limited in size and scope. The states handled everything else from schooling on down. Nowadays, you can't even brush your teeth without having the federal government somehow regulating it. Some may claim "it's for our own good," but to me it sounds like totalitarianism.

People, we must get a hold of this mess and return to sensible limited government! We must demand a balanced budget amendment where government spending is limited to a percentage of GPD not balanced by raising taxes. We must pay off the national debt. And, we must get rid of the Federal Reserve Bank system. I have been appalled at how uninformed and apathetic everyone is on all this. Don't most people operate on a budget for their household expenses? Don't they balance income with outgo, all the while trying to set some funds aside for savings and emergencies? Certainly this is what any responsible person would do, and so should a responsible country. When your income goes down, it's time to tighten up your belt and cut down on spending? A credit card has always tempted people to overspend and this is exactly what the US government is doing and will continue to do unless we put a stop to it. We must yank away their credit card. This "independent" Federal Banking system, which is far from being independent as they claim, is a partner in crime with the federal government's robbery of our hard-earned assets. They do everything possible to accommodate and perpetuate the federal government's spendthrift insanity. Of course, if we do what is required to fix this mess, there will be all kinds of people upset, but never is a major surgery to fix a life-threatening situation a pleasant experience. You do it or you die. We need to take the medicine and fix it.

I absolutely abhor the Federal Reserve Board (Fed), just as I detest their smug attitude of superiority. They act as if they know what in the hell they are doing. If that be true, then they are all "enemies of the state" since they are destroying the US economy, stripping the value of the dollar, and confiscating the value of people's assets on purpose. Normally thieves are thrown into jail and traitors shot. They have decreased the value of the dollar by allowing inflation and most recently dumping some **3.5 trillion** unearned dollars into the economy with their QE (quantitative easing) BS. They don't believe in the free-market system and its ability to rectify a downturn. The Fed has followed in the footsteps of FDR, who by intervening in the economy thinking he was smarter than the markets, made the 1929 Great Depression 3 times worse and prolonged it some 10 years.

In truth, the Fed's actions are all part of the ongoing deliberate plan to pay back the government's debts with dollars of a lesser value via inflation. It is disguised robbery. Anyone who was diligent enough to work hard and save a little bit has seen the value of those dollars drastically degraded. $1.00 from 1990 is now only worth only $0.50 in 2016. "*Inflation is the one form of taxation that can be imposed without legislation.*" – Milton Friedman

A quick simplistic demonstration of how this happens. Let's say our total economy is composed of 100 loaves of bread (LB),

100 workers who make $1 day, and $100. In this economy, one LB is worth $1. Now suppose the money printer (government thru Fed) comes along and adds $3.00 to the money supply without any increase in the amount of LB produced, we would now have $103 chasing 100 LB. That move raises the value of a single LB to $1.03 or, in reverse thinking, the purchasing power of $1 has decreased by 3%. The workers still make $1 day so now it takes them more than a day to purchase 1 LB. This sly little move pays big benefits to the government who now is able to pay back their earlier $1 debt with money that is worth less in real terms. Instead of paying off the real value of their original $1 debt they do it with a $1 that is worth 3% less (97 cents). Believe it or not, this is exactly what the Fed shoots for – they want 2 to 3% inflation per year or, better said, they want the dollar to devalue at 2 to 3% per year. Sad thing is that the general public is being screwed because their wages are not pegged to this inflation rate, but you can rest assured the wages of the money printer (government) certainly are. After all, they are the ones perpetrating this trick. So while the earnings of the general public are decreasing in real value, the money printer is immune (yet boy does he sympathize with the poor folks who are suffering.) This robbery has occurred since the dollar's value was taken off the gold standard in 1933. Freeing it from being pegged to the value of a set commodity allowed the money printer to change the value of a dollar bill simply by printing more/less of them. It would be damn near impossible to go back to the gold standard now, but if adding money to the money supply was only allowed when there is an increase in LB (GDP) the value of money would stay constant. So if 3 new LBs were added to the economy, adding $3 to the money supply would have kept everything level. $103 = 103 LB. Now suppose the money printers thinking that they can stimulate the bakers to produce more LB throws another $100 into the money supply. We find that they

have done little more than doubled the price of LB (for now $200 is chasing 100 LB), and confused the marketplace with their absurdity. Of course, my example here is very simplistic, but it does show that a stable money supply is very important to protect the value of workers' wages, and also that production should drive the money supply. It does not work the other way around. If the amount of new dollars printed was pegged to an increase or decrease in GDP (goods produced), the value of the dollar would be stable, inflation would disappear, and we could do away with the Fed.

The Fed has further attacked the economy and the American people by forcing the interest rate to stay at or near zero in recent years (2008–??). Somehow, in their perverted minds, they figured this would stimulate businesses to borrow cheaply and invest the borrowed capital in business growth and the economy would magically "get all better." Trouble is the Fed failed to recall that it is not cheap money that drives a business's success, but folks buying their goods. This "zero" interest plan of theirs also decimates your personal savings. Since the bankers are now able to get all the money they want from the Feds for "free," why should they pay you any interest. None of this trash worked in the Great Depression, but they decided to try it again anyway. They said that "the reason it didn't work well then was because the infusion of cash wasn't large enough." Einstein said, "Insanity is doing the same thing over and over again and expecting different results." Need I say more about leftists who will never accept that their thinking is irreparably flawed? The Fed is in cahoots with the federal government to keep the interest rate unnaturally low so service on the National Debt stays as small as possible. If the interest rate was allowed to float as it should – it would be much higher, of course – and the federal government would be forced to shell out more dough to pay interest on the National Debt. Just a 1% upward tick in the interest rate means an additional outlay of $20 billion in interest payments for the year to service the $20 trillion debt!

While we are talking about the federal deficit – what do a normal people do when they can't pay their debts? They sell off assets until they have none left or the government comes in and does it for them. So why won't the US government do the same thing to pay their own bills? They already illegally own a pile of state lands for reasons not named in the Constitution. Selling this land would give them the chance to "kill two birds with one stone." First, it would raise funds to pay down the federal debt, and second it would return the land to its rightful owners. I would personally like for the US government to just give it back to the states without a sale, but we both know that is unlikely to happen.

Not only do I personally support a balanced budget amendment, an unmovable federal debt limit, dissolving the Fed, pegging an increase in the money supply to the GDP, but I also would like to see the balanced budget amendment written in such a way that total federal government income be tied to a percentage of GDP (like 7%), and also a time limit set to pay off any debt. This would place much more pressure on the legislators to do what is right for the country's economy rather than catering to environmental and other special interest activists as they do now. Funny how one looks at things differently when it affects your own pocket book.

Foreign Affairs

I HAVE ALREADY MENTIONED THAT we must stop getting in wars all over the planet, but how about alliances with other countries? In President George Washington's farewell address of 1796 he urged the US government to "*steer clear of permanent alliances with any portion of the foreign world*." He acknowledged that, while temporary alliances during "extraordinary emergencies" may be required, we should remain neutral and focus on our own affairs. This counsel, like many others he gave, has gone totally unheeded. Today, the USA is involved in long-lasting military alliances with 28 countries in Europe (NATO), plus Japan, Philippines, Korea, Taiwan, Australia, New Zealand, that I am aware of. All these alliances should be rethought along the lines of whether it is needed for **our** defense or not. Seems to me they are all the other way around – to secure other people's security. We are just getting used. These countries may need us, but we most certainly don't need them. If they want protection – pay up.

> "I cannot undertake to lay my finger on that article in the federal Constitution which granted a right to Congress of expending, on objects of benevolence, the money of their constituents."
> – James Madison

Next, we must discuss this monumental disaster that is called the "United Nations." We should not spend another microsecond as a member of this farce. What started as a "pie in the sky" idea now serves only to fleece wealth from the USA to other countries. Some $9.2 billion was sent by US taxpayers in 2016 to the UN and its various organizations (www.state.gov). I would say "dido" to stopping all these USA government foreign aid outlays as well. Out of the 195 counties on the planet, the USA is sending over $36 billion annually in aid to 142 of them (www.state.gov). In other words, not only do we have an out-of-control welfare problem at home (35% of the population are users – 2012 Census), but the USA is also providing welfare handouts to over 73% of the world. It is not the job of the US government to take care of foreign countries. Its job is to care for its own citizens. They should never be able to take our hard-earned money and simply give it to another nation. The US government can't even pay its own bills (remember the $20 trillion hole we are in), yet we continue to augment this debt with asinine policies like foreign welfare. Foreign aid is something that should be handled by nongovernmental organizations and financed through private donations. This is not to exclude short-term emergency foreign help in case of a natural disaster when approved by the people (Congress). Our foreign aid has been used as a carrot to influence a country's political regime to follow a certain behavior, but this moronic policy has failed to do anything except create a never-ending "squeaky wheel" syndrome. According to the Cato Institute, "Since the 1960s, sub-Saharan Africa has received nearly $500 billion in aid, yet the region has become poorer in the past several decades." The Cato Institute's analysis found that aid spending in Africa is a reverse incentive to its development. And, as always, a good portion of this "aid" finds its way into the pockets of the country's corrupt politicians.

Last, we should never enter into a treaty or partnership of any type that lessens the independence and sovereignty of the USA or subjects her citizenry to control from anyone other than constitutionally elected government officials. This would be to say that accords like NAFTA, the Trans-Pacific Partnership, or the Paris Climate Agreement (the fleece USA and redistribute accord), should never ever see the light of day.

Closure

THERE IS A BUNCH of other political hotbed issues being tossed around that I could comment on, but to me, most are totally absurd. This LGBT stuff is laughable. If you have a penis use the men's bathroom, if you have a vagina use the women's bathroom. If you can't figure that out, then go pee on a tree and see a shrink. As a last-ditch effort, one could always look on their birth certificate and if still in denial, maybe it is best to go get a blood test in order to check your sex chromosomes (XX or XY).

This left-wing push for socialized medicine is another easy one. Anybody with half a brain knows that all throughout world history, wherever socialism has been tried it has failed, yet many here in the USA, who know absolutely nothing of history, are so delusional they believe that by some miracle it will work this time in the US medical industry. Take it from me, one who has lived under socialized medicine in foreign countries – it is a frigging disaster. The best costs and best care will always be produced from a free market with open competition not some government-mandated and -supported monopoly. Such a system only produces corruption, long waits, poor service, and few choices. I reckon some folks may delight in waking up before dawn in order to race down and stand in a long line for hours just to get a number to be seen, then with that number in hand waiting for many more hours until it's your turn to be seen by the doctor they assign you. These same folks must think it is really efficient to waste a whole day to spend 10 minutes with a doctor. Then again, they may also enjoy being put on an 8- to 12-month waiting list for a needed surgery or even being rejected from having it based on age or condition. Many Third World countries have two medical systems, one a government-sponsored public system where an individual can opt in by paying a monthly subscription fee or they can simply pay per usage, and the other is a private free-market system. You choose which one you want to use depending on your personal finances or desire at the moment. Many use a combination of both. If the US illegal immigration situation is corrected, welfare abuse curtailed, hospital emergency room care only given for real life-threatening emergencies instead of for the sniffles, tort reform addressed, and the free market opened up, we would see a precipitous drop in our medical costs.

If you are interested in any of the subjects I have presented please use the references I have listed as a springboard for your own study. I would also recommend to all who want to gain a better understanding on political themes, economics, the Constitution, or American history to sign up for the free on-line courses offered by Hillsdale College (www.hillsdale.edu). They are a great resource. While I believe many of the "fixer upper" type ideas that I have shared could be legislated by Congress and signed into law by the president, some of these ideas might be best handled as a Constitutional amendment to cement them more firmly as part of our founding principles (balanced budget, clarifying birthright citizenship, undoing popular election of senators, term limiting judges, etc.). Besides that, to find a Congress who will curb their own overreach may be a difficult task. With 70% of the state legislatures currently controlled by conservative legislatures (11/2016) the time is nearing when a Constitutional convention could become a reality (need 75% state approval). In addition to some of the possible Constitutional amendments that I have suggested, Texas governor Greg Abbot recently unveiled the "Texas Plan" which is a list of 9 Constitutional Amendments that would clearly limit federal intrusion into state functions and help move us back to a true Republic. They are:

1. Prohibit Congress from regulating activity that occurs wholly within one state.
2. Require Congress to balance its budget.
3. Prohibit administrative agencies—and the unelected bureaucrats that staff them—from creating federal law.
4. Prohibit administrative agencies—and the unelected bureaucrats that staff them—from preempting state law.
5. Allow a two-thirds majority of the states to override a US Supreme Court decision.
6. Require a seven-justice supermajority vote for US Supreme Court decisions that invalidate a democratically enacted law.
7. Restore the balance of power between the federal and state governments by limiting the former to the powers expressly delegated to it in the Constitution.
8. Give state officials the power to sue in federal court when federal officials overstep their bounds.
9. Allow a two-thirds majority of the states to override a federal law or regulation.

"The ultimate result of shielding men from the effects of folly is to fill the world with fools."   – Herbert Spencer

www.ingramcontent.com/pod-product-compliance
Lightning Source LLC
Chambersburg PA
CBHW022122280326
41933CB00007B/509